WILD F

AND WHERE

IN NORTHE

VOLUME THREE

Acid Uplands

WILD FLOWERS
AND WHERE TO FIND THEM
IN NORTHERN ENGLAND

VOLUME THREE

Acid Uplands

LAURIE FALLOWS

FRANCES LINCOLN

A pocket guide to the wild flowers of Northern England, their historical, folk-mythological and medicinal attributes, with some background essays on related topics ❀ When and where to find them, their identifying features and flowering periods ❀ Detailed self-guided walks with simple maps to facilitate discovery

Volume 3
Acid Uplands
Mountain, moorland and acid heaths

Also in this series
Volume 1
Northern Limestone
Limestone meadows, pastures and woods

Volume 2
Waterside Ways
Streamsides, pond margins, bog and coastal areas

Frances Lincoln Ltd
4 Torriano Mews
Torriano Avenue
London NW5 2RZ
www.franceslincoln.com

ISBN 0 7112 2028 X

Origination by Imagescan, Malaysia
Printed in China by C S Graphics

Half-title page: (top) Broom; (centre) Starry Saxifrage; (bottom) Heath Spotted Orchid
Title pages: Easedale Crag and Tarn

CONTENTS

Introduction   7
  Wild plants and the law   9
How to use the flower directory   10
  Abbreviations   11
  Botanical terms   12

Geology of the region   13
  Map   14
  Time chart   17
Moorland vegetation   20

Flower directory   22
Seasonal flowering charts   24
114 of the region's plants   28

Walks   88
Map symbols   90
16 spectacular discovery walks   91

Further reading   126
Index of plant names   127

Acknowledgements

I would like to express my heartfelt thanks to my wife Hazel, for her patience, support and understanding; to my daughter Jane and grandson Andrew for their invaluable assistance in the hitherto dark realms of computer wizardry; to my other daughter Gay and friend Joyce Langtree for assistance with fieldwork and walk-planning.

I would like to dedicate these three volumes to my late mother Mary, née Vickers, for stimulating my initial interest in the flowers that played such an important part in her life, especially in her native Corbridge on Tyne, Northumberland.

LF
Windermere
2003

INTRODUCTION

For over fifty years I have conducted guided walks for National Park and local government authorities, and for educational and recreational organisations in the Yorkshire Dales, the Lake District, the Cheviots, the Galloway Hills of southern Scotland, and Snowdonia. I have introduced many thousands of adults and occasionally schoolchildren to the countryside, stressing not only the physical enjoyment of the great outdoors but also an understanding of its scenery, its history and its wildlife.

The information most frequently requested concerned the identification, the habitats, the folklore, the culinary and medicinal uses of plants, and simple field guides to help with their recognition. As more and more people take quiet recreation in country walks, the need for simple, descriptive, illustrated guides to wild flowers has increased. Existing flower guides have a number of drawbacks for beginners. They often rely on a knowledge of botanical terms, and do not indicate where particular species may be found. Furthermore, most of those that give flowering periods relate to central and southern England, whereas in the north of the country the climate, altitude and latitude often delay flowering by several weeks.

The plants covered in these books are of course not specific to the region, but can be found in other regions with similar soils and climates throughout the rest of Britain and Europe, making these guides of universal value.

Descriptions are stated in the simplest terms, and do not require any knowledge of the technical vocabulary of botanists. Read in association with the colour photographs, they should prevent confusion and make for certain identification. The flowering charts are based on regular personal observation throughout the year, and should provide an accurate record of when to see the plants in flower in northern England.

The walks are located in the Lake District and Southern Lakeland, the Yorkshire Dales, and Upper Teesdale. The straightforward instructions are

Eskdale

illustrated by specially drawn, simple maps, with a note of the relevant Ordnance Survey maps for those who want further cartographical information. Distances are given in kilometres, miles and average times. While some of the walks are longer than others, the maps often show how they may be shortened. Occasionally, fairly steep gradients and rough or boggy terrain will be encountered – where appropriate, these factors are mentioned.

RESPECT FOR HABITATS

All the plants featured in this book have been recorded within two metres of public or permissive footpaths. If the walk guides are followed, there is no risk of trespass. Remember to tread carefully and avoid trampling plants when looking at or photographing them, especially rare species.

Plants must never be picked or uprooted. Apart from being illegal (see box, page 9), removing them detracts from the natural environment.

WILD PLANTS AND THE LAW

All plants growing in the wild and their habitats are protected by the Wildlife and Countryside Act, 1981. Section 13 states: 'It is an offence for anyone to intentionally pick, uproot or destroy any wild plant on schedule 8,' which includes, among others, Spring Gentians, Bluebells, Pennyroyal, Teesdale Sandwort, Slender Naiad and some ferns, lichens and mosses. European legislation embodied in Conservation (Natural Habitats, etc.) Regulations 1994 adds further plants including Lady's Slipper Orchid, Shore Dock and Yellow Marsh Saxifrage. Section 13 (1)(b) of the 1981 Act states: 'it is an offence for any unauthorised person to intentionally uproot *any* wild plant,' – i.e., whether it is protected or not. Dealing in wild plants is forbidden under Section13 (2) (9a), which makes it an offence to 'sell, offer or expose for sale or possess or transport for the purpose of sale, or advertisement of intent to sell, any live or dead wild plant (or any part of or anything derived from such a plant) on schedule 8.'

Section 4 (3) of the Theft Act 1968 states that the picking of wild flowers, fruit or fungi for reward is considered to be theft. Uprooting a whole plant may also be considered theft. In Scotland, damage to flowers or plants on someone's property may be punishable as vandalism under the Criminal Law (Consolidation) (Scotland) Act 1995, Section 52, or as the common law crime of malicious mischief.

CONSUMPTION

The herbal uses described in this guide are for general interest only. Plants and plant extracts must not be applied to the skin or taken internally without reference to a qualified herbalist or at least an up-to-date herbal. Very careful identification is essential before any kind of experiment. Even in recent times, people have died through incorrect identification of plants – for example, by confusing Foxglove leaves with Comfrey. Identification should be by examining the whole plant, not just the flower or the leaf alone, since there are many superficial similarities.

HOW TO USE THE
FLOWER DIRECTORY

The plants are grouped according to the main colours of their flowers. However, many may be present in different colours – for example, Mountain Pansies are normally yellow in the Dales, but more likely to be blue or purple in Teesdale; Milkwort varies from blue or pink to white. Flower colour should be only one factor in identifying a species.

CHARTS

The Directory is preceded by colour charts, showing the months in which the plants may be seen in flower in northern England. Colours can vary considerably, even within species, so this should be taken as only a rough guide to aid identification. For simplification, and because colour is often subjective, the charts include some flowers that fit only marginally into the given colour categories.

While the charts are a general guide to flowering times in Northern England, individual specimens may flower outside these months. This may be because of peculiar local conditions, or because some species flower in profusion for a month or two and then produce a second flush later in the year. Groundsel, Chickweed and Red Campion may be seen virtually all the year round.

The charts are original, and have been compiled over six years by personal observation throughout the year. Flowering times may therefore vary from those published in other guides, many of which describe lower latitudes and altitudes. However, the region does range from the mild, moist southern Lakeland through the drier and higher Yorkshire Dales to the wet high altitude of Upper Teesdale, so variation is inevitable.

PHOTOGRAPHS

Each species is illustrated by a colour photograph, showing the general appearance of
the plant, and the shape and relative size of
its leaves and flowers. Please note that the
scale of the individual photographs is not
consistent.

NAMES

The main regional vernacular name is given
first, then any other names in common use.
Where there are many alternative names,
only a selection is given. Vernacular names

ABBREVIATIONS

aka	also known as
Arab	Arabic
AS	Anglo-Saxon
Celt	Celtic
Fr	French
Ger	German
Gk	Greek
L	Latin
ODan	Old Danish
OE	Old English
OFr	Old French
ON	Old Norse

can be confusing. In different parts of the country, a single flower can have
many different names – Cuckoo Pint, for example, has at least ninety
recorded local names. The name Thunderflower is used for both Wood
Anemone and Wood Cranesbill; Aaron's Rod for Agrimony and Great
Mullein. The Bluebell of England becomes the Hyacinth in parts of Scotland, and their Bluebell is the English Harebell. Latin names are therefore
also given to aid precise identification. Wherever possible, the origin and
explanation of both Latin and common names are also expounded.

HEIGHT AND FLOWERING MONTHS

When identifying a plant do not refer just to the photograph, but also to the
height in the written description.

DESCRIPTION

The first paragraph describes general characteristics. The second paragraph
gives particulars of where the plant grows, and an indication of its place in
folklore and in folk and contemporary medicine.

IDENTIFICATION TIPS

When trying to identify a plant you do not know, it is important to consider
all its features – particularly the shape of both flower and leaves, whether or

BOTANICAL TERMS

Every effort has been made to keep plant descriptions as simple as possible, but a few botanical terms are unavoidable.

alternate arranged alternately up the stem

annual completing a full life cycle in one year

anthers cases on top of stamens that contain pollen

basal just above ground level at the foot of the stem

biennial forming a rosette of basal leaves the first year; raising a stem, flowering and dying in the second year

bract small, leaf-like organ on flower stem

calyx sepals at flower base, often joined in a cup or tube

deciduous shedding leaves in the autumn

floret individual flower in a tight arrangement, as in Daisy

labiate in two parts, like lips

lanceolate lance-shaped

leaflet one division of a compound leaf

lobed divided into sections

node place on stem where leaves arise

ovary the seed container below the style

perennial going on year after year with incremental vegetative increase

persistent leaves overwinter on plant

petals inner leaves, often highly coloured, of flower heads

pinnate divided into leaflets either side of stalk

raceme flower spike

rhizome swollen underground root that feeds the plant

sepals outer leaves of flower buds and holders of flower

stamens male pollen-bearing organs

stigma top of the style that receives the pollen

stipules small leaf-like appendages at the base of leaf stalks

stolons creeping stems that produce new plant stems at intervals

style tube or stalk between stigma and ovary

trefoil with three leaflets, as in Clover

tubers swollen underground organs with plant food

wintergreen retaining old leaves over winter

not parts are hairy, whether it is growing in dry or wet conditions, in sun or in shade, and whether it is shunned or devoured by livestock. Consider its situation in relation to the type of ground it is growing in and its association with other plant life. Climate and altitude can also cause considerable variation. The walks section gives further information about when and where to locate certain species.

A small hand lens of 10× magnification is very helpful in identification, and also reveals the hidden beauties of diminutive species.

GEOLOGY OF THE REGION

Plant life varies in any region by virtue of the soil, the altitude, the climate and, over the past ten thousand years, the impact of man and his farming activities. In general terms, with the exception of lower areas blanketed by river-borne silts or glacial deposits, or wet uplands carpeted by peat, soils tend to reflect the underlying rocks from which they derive. It is not relevant to this brief survey to discuss the origins and development of the very oldest volcanic rocks in the region. Suffice it to say that they form the crust of the earth on which were superimposed newer rocks created by the deposition of their eroded silts and sands or animal remains, and by volcanic intrusions.

ACID UPLANDS GEOLOGY

During the second half of the twentieth century, geologists came to realise that the earth's crust was made up of seven major and several smaller, slow-moving, floating masses, or plates of rock. Their movement in relation to one another, caused by convection currents within the underlying mantle, created earthquakes and volcanoes, and raised up mountains and mountain ranges.

Plate tectonics Where two plates collide, one is forced down below its neighbour in a process known as subduction. As it subsides into the earth's hot underzone, it releases energy in the form of earthquakes that crumple the subsiding crust and allow molten magma to erupt in the form of volcanoes along the line of collision.

Where two plates are drawing apart, the crust is torn open, creating a weakness that permits hot magma to force its way through as more volcanoes. In each case, molten rock explodes over the surrounding surface and

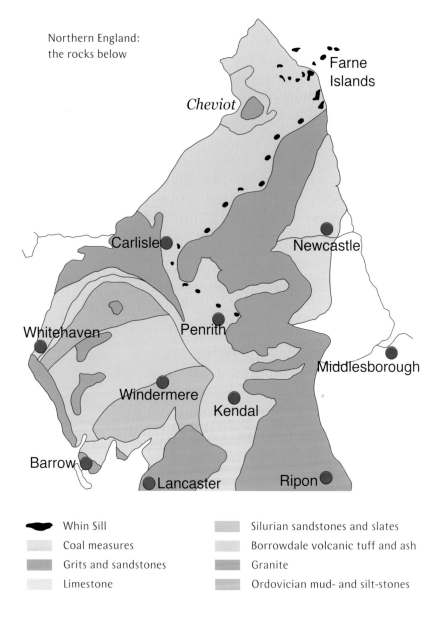

Northern England:
the rocks below

Farne Islands

Cheviot

Carlisle

Newcastle

Whitehaven

Penrith

Middlesborough

Windermere

Kendal

Barrow

Lancaster

Ripon

Whin Sill	Silurian sandstones and slates
Coal measures	Borrowdale volcanic tuff and ash
Grits and sandstones	Granite
Limestone	Ordovician mud- and silt-stones

deposits both lava and ash over a wide distance, while rock-forming magma is intruded into the underground crust.

Volcanic rocks   Above the surface, the atmosphere or sea quickly cools the deposits, which form into three main types of rock:

Basalt is a dark, heavy, fine-textured rock, a lava solidified too quickly to crystallise. Its main elements are pyroxene, olivine and feldspar.

Andesite is also solidified lava, more acid than basalt and lighter in colour, containing feldspar and pyroxene. It is named after the Andes Mountains.

Rhyolite comes from a more acid lava, mainly quartz and feldspar, lighter in weight and colour, with prominent quartz crystals.

Volcanic ash contains small or large fragments of shattered rock; scattered over the land surrounding volcanoes, it consolidates into a rock called **tuff**, which can be fine- or coarse-grained and may be made up of light angular pebbles in a darker matrix, called **breccia**. Mesolithic man used a flinty kind of tuff from Langdale for stone axes.

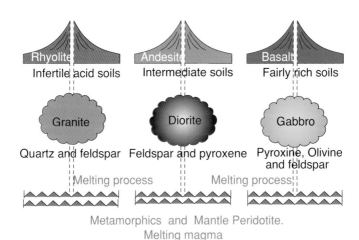

Rhyolite	Andesite	Basalt
Infertile acid soils	Intermediate soils	Fairly rich soils
Granite	Diorite	Gabbro
Quartz and feldspar	Feldspar and pyroxene	Pyroxine, Olivine and feldspar
Melting process		Melting process

Metamorphics and Mantle Peridotite.
Melting magma

Plutonic rocks These are new rocks formed by the sub-surface intrusion of slow-cooling magma. They include granites and other crystalline forms.

Granite is a hard, crystalline rock consisting of glass-like quartz, large white crystals of feldspar and flakes of mica. It can vary in colour, but in the Lake District it is generally pinkish. It is an underground production, and can be seen only where erosion of the overlying rocks has exposed it. Like its surface equivalent basalt, granite has a high silica content, which produces a relatively infertile soil.

Diorite is a coarse-grained rock consisting principally of feldspar and pyroxene. The plutonic equivalent of andesite, it degrades into a more fertile soil than granite.

Gabbro is dark and heavy, more coarse-grained than granite, free of quartz and consists mainly of feldspar and augite. Like granite, it is an underground equivalent of basalt, but is relatively short of silica and therefore breaks down into a fairly rich soil.

During the latter part of the Carboniferous period, subterranean volcanic activity in the region released molten magma into the upper layers of lime-

Langdale Pikes from Loughrigg Tarn

GEOLOGICAL TIME CHART

Period	million yrs ago	Location	Origin
Carboniferous			
Whin Sill	295	Under N Pennines	Volcanic
Millstone Grit	300	Central Pennines	Deltaic
Coal Measures	310	W Cumberland, Durham and Northumberland	Swamp
Yoredale Series		Yorkshire Dales	Cyclic deposition
Great Limestone	345	S and E of Lakes	Marine skeletons
Caledonian Uplift	410	Lakes and Pennines	Volcanic
Silurian	450	South Lakes	Deep ocean silt
Borrowdale Volcanics	460	Central Lakes	Volcanic
Ordovician	510	North Lakes	Deep sea mud

stone and sandstone. It formed a thick slab right across the north-east of England, from the western Pennines to the Northumbrian coast, from Teesdale in the south to the Farne Islands in the north. The rock it slowly hardened into is called **whinstone** or **quartz-dolerite**. It is mainly acid, but close proximity to limestone can enrich its soils to allow a varied flora. So, even in volcanic areas, there can be a wide range of soils and plant habitats.

Bogs and tarns The impervious nature of all volcanic rocks restricts the drainage of surface water, which accumulates in hollows to form lakes, tarns and boggy areas. This water, strongly acidic, hosts little in the way of plants, except where alkaline streams feed into it. Mosses, especially Sphagnum, build up in the bogs, and their decaying humus turns into peat, which can support only a limited number of acid-tolerant plants and sub-shrubs.

SEDIMENTARY ROCKS

Other acid uplands were created by mainly marine deposition. This region exposes little very old rock (see Volume 1, *Northern Limestone*), so this account can start from the Ordovician period.

Ordovician period   During this time, from about five hundred million to three hundred million years ago, earlier volcanoes eroded fairly rapidly; their debris, in the form of mud and silt, was poured into the tropical oceans where it built up to great depths. Its own weight, and that of subsequent inundations, compressed it into mudstones and siltstones: these are the **Skiddaw Slates**. Relatively soft, they have been eroded in time into smooth, sloping fells, but the high acidity of the rock is not conducive to a varied plant population. Like the volcanic rocks, they are impervious to water and allow the creation of highly acid bogs and tarns, with a limited and sometimes habitat-specialised flora.

Silurian period   Following the rock production known as the **Borrowdale Volcanics**, the surrounding land subsided and the rapid erosion of young volcanic rocks poured sand and silt into the surrounding seas. This consolidated over time into the sandstones and shale of **South Lakeland** and the **Howgill Fells**. The soils they break down into are slightly less acidic than those of the Ordovician period. Their calcium content, along with penetration by lime-rich streams, allows a reasonable variety of vegetation. However, the impervious nature of the rocks leads to the formation of bogs and tarns; some of these, not enriched by alkaline becks or flushes, are acid.

Late Carboniferous period   Around three hundred million years ago, the build-up of limestone, sandstone and shales in tropical lagoons, typified by the **Yoredale series** which laid the foundations of the stepped valleys of the Dales, brought the rock level to the surface. Around the massive river mouths, deltas of sand and round pebbles of quartz built up. In time, these accumulations were compacted into the highly acid **Millstone Grits** that now cap **Cross Fell** and the Yorkshire peaks of **Whernside, Ingleborough** and **Pen-y-Ghent**. Eroding into a sandy acid soil, they bear a limited flora; and because of poor drainage, they carry a lot of blanket bog peat and small tarns.

Opposite: Aira Force

MOORLAND VEGETATION

There are broadly three different types of moorland, depending on the depth of peat on the surface and its relative dryness. The highest bogs host Bilberry, Crowberry and Cloudberry, while around ponds are reeds, Horse-tails, Cranberry, Bogbean and Bog Rosemary. Most of the moorland in the region is situated on the northern Pennines, where grouse moors are still maintained. Those in old Lakeland have long since degenerated, largely through over-grazing by sheep.

HEATHER MOOR

This is the driest. It is underlain by peat, often on sloping ground which helps drainage, and is mostly managed as grouse moor. Its principal vegetation consists of Ling, Bell Heather and Bilberry, with lesser colonies of Cross-leaved Heath, Crowberry and Cranberry (on Sphagnum Moss hummocks) in company with Mat Grass, Purple Moor Grass, Heath Rush, Bracken, Hard Fern and several other mosses.

The heathers are burnt between 1 October and 15 April in selected patches at intervals of 7–15 years, to provide plants at different levels of maturity in the grouse habitat. New young growth – from deep, woody roots unaffected by the burning and from seeds lying dormant in the peat – provides food for the birds and their chicks. Older denser areas are ideal for nesting and rearing chicks, the oldest and tallest woody patches providing concealment from predatory foxes, hawks and crows. Sheep help the management of the heather by grazing on the new shoots, but over-grazing (encouraged by agricultural subsidies based on the number of animals in a herd) allows the ingress of bracken. Such degeneration reduces the moor's value for grouse rearing.

Butterwort (*Pinguicula vulgaris*; page 71), Sundew (*Drosera rotundifolia*; page 49) and Mosses

BILBERRY MOOR

This lies over deeper peat, usually on higher ground in the Pennines. Its vegetation indicator is the Bog Bilberry (*Vaccinium uligonosum*), which can survive in the wetter, poorly drained conditions. This grows in association with Ling, Cross-leaved Heath, Bilberry, Crowberry and Bog Asphodel.

COTTON GRASS MOOR

Found in areas of high rainfall on the deepest, most saturated peat, this sustains only those plants that can survive the absence of oxygen and minerals around their roots. The commonest of these is Cotton Grass, whose creeping rhizomes contain air canals.

Some plants have developed the capacity to abstract oxygen and minerals from insects – these include Butterwort and Sundew, which grow in wet places and entrap flies to supply their nutritional needs by means of sticky hairs. Sphagnum and other mosses also grow here, with new peat continually forming from their decaying remains.

Overleaf: Bell Heather (*Erica cinerea*; page 53) on Beacon Fell

21

PLANTS IN FLOWER	Jan	Feb	Mar	Apr	May	June	July	Aug	Sep	Oct	Nov	Dec
Archangel, Yellow												
Asphodel, Bog												
Bartsia, Yellow												
Broom												
Corydalis, Climbing												
Cow Wheat												
Gorse												
Lady's Mantle, Alpine												
Pimpernel, Yellow												
Rose Root												
St John's Wort, Trailing												
Saxifrage, Golden												
Saxifrage, Yellow Mountain												
Sedge, Spring												
Spearwort, Lesser												
Tormentil												
Tutsan												

PLANTS IN FLOWER	Jan	Feb	Mar	Apr	May	June	July	Aug	Sep	Oct	Nov	Dec
Broomrape, Common						▓	▓	▓	▓			

PLANTS IN FLOWER	Jan	Feb	Mar	Apr	May	June	July	Aug	Sep	Oct	Nov	Dec
Angelica, Wild												
Avens, Mountain												
Bedstraw, Heath												
Bedstraw, Hedge												
Bedstraw, Marsh												
Bistort, Alpine												
Blinks												
Bogbean												
Cotton Grass												
Cress, Thale												
Goosegrass												
Parnassus, Grass of												
Pennywort												
Pennywort, Marsh												
Pepper, Water												
Sandwort, Fine-Leaved												
Sandwort, Three-Veined												
Saxifrage, Mossy												
Saxifrage, Starry												
Scurvygrass												
Sneezewort												
Stitchwort, Lesser												
Stitchwort, Marsh												
Stitchwort, Wood												
Stonecrop, English												
Sundew												
Sundew, Oblong-Leaved												
Yarrow												

PLANTS IN FLOWER	Jan	Feb	Mar	Apr	May	June	July	Aug	Sep	Oct	Nov	Dec
Burdock, Lesser							█	█	█			
Burnet, Great						█	█	█	█			
Cinquefoil, Marsh					█	█	█	█				
Foxglove						█	█	█				
Heather, Bell						█	█	█	█			
Knapweed						█	█	█	█			
Ling							█	█	█			
Lobelia, Water							█	█				
Orchid, Northern Marsh						█	█	█				
Pansy, Mountain					█	█	█	█				
Rosemary, Bog					█	█	█	█				
Speedwell, Heath					█	█	█	█				
Thistle, Creeping							█	█	█			
Thistle, Marsh							█	█	█			
Thistle, Spear							█	█	█	█		
Toadflax, Ivy-Leaved					█	█	█	█	█			
Violet, Marsh				█	█	█	█					
Willowherb, Rose Bay							█	█	█			
Woundwort, Marsh						█	█	█	█			

PLANTS IN FLOWER	Jan	Feb	Mar	Apr	May	June	July	Aug	Sep	Oct	Nov	Dec
Bartsia, Alpine							█	█				
Bilberry				█	█							
Bindweed, Field						█	█	█	█			
Butterbur			█	█								
Cowberry				█	█	█						
Cranberry					█	█						
Crowberry				█	█							
Heath, Cross-Leaved						█	█	█				
Lousewort				█	█	█	█					
Lousewort, Marsh				█	█	█	█					
Orchid, Heath Spotted					█	█	█					
Orpine							█	█	█			
Parsley, Hedge						█	█	█				
Pimpernel, Bog						█	█	█				
Ragged Robin					█	█	█					
Redshank						█	█	█	█	█		
Valerian, Marsh					█	█	█	█				
Willowherb, Marsh						█	█	█				
Willowherb, New Zealand						█	█	█				

PLANTS IN FLOWER	Jan	Feb	Mar	Apr	May	June	July	Aug	Sep	Oct	Nov	Dec
Brooklime					■	■	■	■	■			
Butterwort					■	■		■				
Forget-Me-Not, Water					■	■	■	■	■			
Lungwort			■	■	■							
Milkwort, Heath					■	■	■					
Scabious, Devil's Bit							■	■	■			
Sheepsbit					■	■	■	■				

PLANTS IN FLOWER	Jan	Feb	Mar	Apr	May	June	July	Aug	Sep	Oct	Nov	Dec
Clubmoss, Alpine						■	■	■				
Clubmoss, Fir						■	■	■				
Clubmoss, Lesser						■	■	■				
Clubmoss, Stag's Horn						■	■	■				
Dock, Clustered						■	■	■	■			
Dock, Curled					■	■	■	■				
Miss, Feather				■	■							
Moss, Sphagnum					■	■	■					
Moss, Star						■	■					
Myrtle, Bog				■	■							
Nettle, Stinging					■	■	■	■				
Plantain, Hoary					■	■	■					
Plantain, Ratstail						■	■	■				
Plantain, Ribwort					■	■	■	■				
Plantain, Sea						■	■	■				
Rush, Soft					■	■	■					
Sorrel, Mountain					■	■	■					
Sorrel, Sheep's					■	■	■					

FERNS, FERTILE	Jan	Feb	Mar	Apr	May	June	July	Aug	Sep	Oct	Nov	Dec
Adder's Tongue					■	■	■	■				
Bracken					■	■	■	■				
Fern, Hard					■	■	■	■				
Fern, Parsley					■	■	■	■				
Polypody					■	■	■	■				

ARCHANGEL, YELLOW

WEASEL SNOUT, YELLOW DEADNETTLE

Height 20–60cm/8–24in May–July

Lamiastrum galeobdolon
L *lamium*, deadnettle; Gk *gale*, weasel;
bdolos, nasty smell
Archangel after Archangel Michael, on whose
day (29 September) deadnettles are still in
flower

Hairy perennial with long creeping stolons
that create large patches in woods and
waysides. Hairy upright square stems bear
opposite pairs of pointed-oval deeply toothed
leaves with many narrow bracts in spaced out
whorls. Unstalked yellow flowers crowd into
leaf axils: erect hooded upper lip, lower lip
3-lobed with brown honey-guides. Seeds are
brown nutlets. Strong-smelling.

Like other deadnettles it was believed to
protect people from evil spirits and spells and
cattle from elf-shot, a magic affliction. Used
by Culpeper for healing sores and ulcers.

ASPHODEL, BOG

MOOR GOLDS (YORKSHIRE),
LANCASHIRE ASPHODEL, MAIDEN HAIR
(LANCASHIRE AND YORKSHIRE)

Height 5–40cm/2–16in July–August

Narthecium ossifragum
Gk *Narthecium*, little rod, i.e. stem;
L *ossifragum*, bone breaker (grows in boggy
ground where sheep suffer from foot rot)

A hairless perennial with a long underground
rhizome that sends up flowering tufts. Fleshy,
lance-shaped, often curved leaves at base;
orange-tinged upper leaves rise close to erect
stem. Loose spikes of fragrant yellow star-like
flowers have 6 petals and 6 stamens with
orange tips. Ripening flower parts turn orange,
bearing capsules of brown seeds. Grows in
bogs and peat.

Poisonous to sheep and cattle, creating
serious kidney problems. Seventeenth-century
Lancashire women used it as a yellow hair dye.

BARTSIA, YELLOW

Height 15–38cm/6–15in ❀ June–September

Parentucellia viscosa
L *Parentucellia*, after the Parentucelli, Pope
Nicholas V; *viscosa*, sticky
Bartsia after Swedish botanist Dr Bartoch,
close friend of Linnaeus who named it

A very hairy annual somewhat similar to
Yellow Rattle and also semi-parasitic in that
it takes some sustenance from neighbouring
grasses. An erect unbranched stem bears
opposite, unstalked, toothed, lance-shaped
leaves. 2-lipped yellow snapdragon-like
flowers are borne in leaf axils, lower lip
3-lobed. Seeds in capsules smaller than
the calyx.

Frequent in S and W England and Ireland,
as also in W Europe, but less common in
N England. Seen particularly in dry coastal
grassland, especially North Walney Island.

BROOM

BESOM

Height up to 260cm/80in ❀ May–June

Cytisus scoparius
Gk *cytisus*, probably a corruption of Cythnus,
an island where it grew; L *scopa*, broom

An erect, deciduous, many-branched shrub.
Slender, hairless, ridged, whippy green twigs
without spines bear small simple or trifoliate
leaves. Leafy spikes have one or two scented
yellow pea-flowers, sometimes tinged red.
Seeds are borne in hairy-edged pods, about
2.5–4cm/1–2in long which turn black and
explode when ripe. Grows in dry acid soils
up to 600m/2,000ft.

Contains sparteine, used for heart and
obstetric conditions, and scoparin, a strong
diuretic. In Elizabethan times the buds were
pickled as capers, and the bark has long been
used in tanning and rope-making. Formerly
known as *Planta-genista*, broom was the
badge of the Plantagenet King Henry II.

CORYDALIS, CLIMBING

Height 20–80cm/8–34in ❀ June–December

Corydalis claviculata
Gk *corydalis*, crested lark (spur resembles);
L *claviculata*, club-shaped, with tendrils

A delicate, straggly, much-branched annual
of acid woodlands, sometimes among bracken.
Many branches bear terminal tendrils for
support from other plants, and simple pale
green leaves in 3–5 segments. Creamy-yellow
vetch-like flowers are borne in loose groups
of six to eight, 2-lipped with short spurs.
Small pea-like pods have 2 or 3 seeds. Quite
common in Cumbria and the northern Dales,
occurring in both deciduous and coniferous
woods and under bracken.

Has had many medicinal uses, including
relief for intestinal conditions, menstrual
pain, and stress. In the thirteenth century
it was used to dispel melancholy.

COW WHEAT

HORSE FLOWER, POVERTY BREAD (ISLE OF
WIGHT)

Height 15–30cm/6–12 in ❀ June–September

Melanpyrum pratense
Gk *melas*, black (seeds), pyros, *wheat*;
L *pratense*, of meadows

A slender, hairy, semi-parasitic annual of
acid oak woods and moorland. Fine, narrow,
pointed, short-stalked leaves are borne in
opposite pairs up slender branching stems.
Pairs of yellow 2-lipped flowers rise from leaf
joints, all facing the same side on each stem.
Seeds carried in beaked capsules. A plant of
acid woods and moorland.

The seeds, when mixed with wheaten flour,
produced black bread. Gerard considered it
of little value except that cow wheat flour
'mightily provoketh venerie'. Some early
writers believed it enabled women to bear
sons.

GORSE

FURZE, WHIN

Height to 24cm/96in ❀ April–June, September–October

Ulex europaeus

L *Ulex*, name given by Pliny, who
recommended it to strain gold out of
mountain streams; *europaeus*, European
AS *gorst*, wasteland

A dense, many-branched shrub which forms
large colonies on grassy wasteland. Its stiff
furrowed stems bear ridged spiny leaves.
Coconut-scented yellow flowers are borne in
ones and twos up the stems, a hairy yellowish
cup cradling orange-yellow peaflowers. Hairy
pods explode when ripe to disperse seeds.
Found up to 300m/1,000ft.

    Culpepper prescribed it for jaundice and
urinary complaints, including gravel. Crushed
plants make good animal fodder. Once used
for hedging, for walking sticks and as a fuel
for bakers, brick-makers and lime-burners.

LADY'S MANTLE, ALPINE

OUR LADY'S MANTLE

Height 5–20cm/2–8in ❀ June–August

Alchemilla alpina
Arab *alkemelych*, alchemist; L *alpina*, alpine

A creeping low perennial rising from a strong
rootstock. The leaves have 5 or 7 divided
finger-like segments and are toothed, grey-
green above, silvery-white below. Flowers
3mm, pale yellowish-green, 4-petalled, borne
in dense clusters on floppy stalks. Common
on higher Lakeland fells on grassland, rocky
ledges and stone walls. Introduced on
W Pennines in 1956.

    No known medical uses except possibly
in place of Alchemilla vulgaris.

PIMPERNEL, YELLOW

Height 2–10cm/1–4in ❀ May–July

WOOD LOOSESTRIFE, STAR FLOWER
(WILTSHIRE), MARY'S CLOVER (IRELAND)

Lysimachia nemorum
After King Lysimachus of Sicily, who
recommended it for treating wounds;
L *nemorum*, of woods
Pimpernel from L *bipinella*, double-winged as
in leaves of Burnets

An evergreen perennial with slender crawling
stems that bear opposite, pointed-oval, pale
green leaves on very short stalks. Slender-
stemmed, saucer-shaped, 5-petalled yellow star-
like flowers rise singly from the main stems.
Grows in damp deciduous woodland and near
water. Can be confused with garden escape
L. nummularia (Creeping Jenny), which has
more rounded leaves, and bowl-shaped flowers.
   Astringent and good for open wounds, its use
is limited, *L. nummularia* being more effective.

ROSE ROOT

Height 15–30cm/6–12in ❀ May–June

CHRISTMAS CHEER, SNOWDON ROSE

Sedum rosea
L *sedere*, to sit (classical name for succulents);
rosea, red-tinged

A short tufted perennial rising from a stout
rhizome. Stem round, hairless, upright,
often tinged purple, bearing alternate paddle-
shaped, broad-toothed, greyish, purple-tinged,
succulent leaves. Clusters of yellow,
5-petalled, star-like flowers crown the tops
of the stems. Male and female flowers on
separate stems. Orange fruits resemble flowers.
Prospers on high mountain ledges and gullies
in central Lakeland and the Cross Fell area.
   Gerard wrote: 'Cut the stock and it gives
out a delicious smell "like the damaske Rose".'
Cultivated in cottage gardens to make rose-
scented water. It is the family badge of the
Gunn clan.

ST JOHN'S WORT, TRAILING

Height 5–10cm/2–4in ❀ June–October

Hypericum humifusum
Gk *hyper*, above; *eikon*, image; L *humifusum*,
spreading on the ground

A creeping hairless perennial of dry, acid or
peaty soils. Thin, wiry spreading stems root
periodically to throw up much-branched
flowering stems which bear opposite pairs
of narrow, ovate, unstalked leaves often with
translucent dots and black marginal glands.
Flowers small, pale yellow, 5-petalled, borne
in loose clusters, sepals with black dots round
the edges. Seeds produced in capsules.

A magic plant, hung above pictures to
keep away devils and fairies. Like Perforated
St John's Wort (*Hypericum perforatum*), it has
red sap, likened to the blood of the beheaded
St John, whose religious order used it to treat
wounds.

SAXIFRAGE, GOLDEN

CREEPING JENNY (SUSSEX), GOLDEN
STONEBREAK (GERRARD, 1874), LADY'S
CUSHION, BUTTERED EGGS (WILTSHIRE)

Height 5–15cm/2–6 in ❀ April–July

Chrysosplenium oppositofolium
Gk *chryso*, golden; *splene*, spleen (referring
to the leaf shape); L *oppositifolium*, opposite-
leaved

A low, creeping, perennial of wet places,
usually on acid soil. Its soft, round, hairy,
sprawling stems root easily to form mats.
Blunt-toothed, roundish, opposite or alternate
leaves on short stalks. Flat, leafy terminal
heads bear few greenish-yellow 4-sepalled
flowers (no petals). Black seeds are formed in
the flower cups. Widespread in damp places.
The less common *C. alternifolium* is similar
but the stem leaves are alternate.

Once used for conditions of the spleen. In
the Vosges it is eaten as a salad named 'cresson
de vâche'.

SAXIFRAGE, YELLOW MOUNTAIN

Height 5–15cm/2–6in ❀ June–August

Saxifraga aizoides
L *saxum*, rock; *frango*, break; *aizoides*, like
Saxifraga aizoon, with branched flowers in
loose clusters

A low, mat-forming perennial, slightly hairy,
with thickish, unstalked, narrow, slightly
toothed, lance-shaped, alternate leaves.
Upright stems bear few, stalked, 5-petalled
flowers with red-spotted petals and red
anthers. The widely separated petals expose
5 green sepals. Pollinated by flies.
   An arctic alpine plant of damp, base-rich
soils. Frequent in the Lake District, Upper
Teesdale and Scotland, but unknown in
Snowdonia. It was first found in Westmorland
by John Ray in 1661.

SEDGE, SPRING

Height 5–15cm/2–6in ❀ April–May

Carex caryophyllea
L *carex*, name for group; *caryo*, nut;
-phyll, leaved

Not technically a flower but a sedge, i.e. a
grass-like plant. Sedges have solid, 3-sided
stems and leaves that form cylinders round
them. Male and female are on different spikes,
the female flowers ripening into small nutlets,
the male bearing yellow pollen. Among the
earliest flowering plants, Spring Sedge is
included in this selection because it is very
prominent among drab grasses in an otherwise
barren time of the year and is sometimes
taken for a flower.
   No known culinary, medicinal or practical
uses.

SPEARWORT, LESSER

BANEWORT

Height 5–50cm/2–20in ❀ May–September

Ranunculus flammula
L *rana*, frog; *flammula*, inflammatory
(referring to the sap)

A hairless, tufted perennial of wet places.
Reddish upright or creeping, rooting stems
bear stalked, oval, lower and unstalked,
lance-shaped upper leaves, sometimes
toothed. Shiny yellow buttercup flowers are
borne singly or in loose clusters. Seeds are in
globular clusters as with other buttercups. It
grows in marsh and beside becks and tarns.

Gerard called it Banewort 'bicause it is
dangerous and deadly for sheepe: and that if
they feed of the same it inflameth their livers,
freeteth and blistereth their guts and entrails',
i.e. it caused liver rot. Medieval beggars are
reputed to have used the sap to raise blisters
and sores on their faces to elicit sympathy
and generosity.

TORMENTIL

BLOOD ROOT (NORTHUMBERLAND),
ENGLISH SARSAPARILLA

Height 5–50cm/2–20in ❀ May–October

Potentilla erecta
L *potens*, powerful (healer); *erecta*, upright;
tormina, torment (pain)

A slender, often prostrate, downy perennial
with a stout woody rootstock. Stalked basal
leaves which usually die before the flowers
appear have 3 toothed leaflets, although bracts
make them look like 5 leaflets. Unstalked
upper leaves are similar. Stalked 4-petalled
yellow flowers carried in loose clusters. Up
to 20 seeds held in a small solid cup.

A highly astringent herb long used for
toothache, diarrhoea, fevers and cholera.
Used as a compress for minor burns, grazes and
sunburn. In Guernsey, a remedy for quinsy and
paralysis. Having more tannin than oak bark,
it was used for tanning hides, and its roots to
yield a red dye.

TUTSAN

SWEET AMBER, TREACLE LEAF (IN CUMBERLAND
TREACLE WAS ONCE A SOVEREIGN REMEDY)

Height 30–90cm/12–36in ✺ June–August

Hypericum androsaemum
Gk *hyper*, above; *eikon*, picture (hung there to
fend off evil spirits); *andros*, man; *haema*, blood
Tutsan from Fr *toute-saine*, all healthy

A hairless, evergreen subshrub of damp woods
and hedges. A woody stock raises erect stems
that soon become woody, bearing opposite
pairs of large, oval, unstalked leaves. Yellow
5-petalled flowers with larger supporting green
sepals are borne in loose terminal clusters.
Berry-like fruits red at first, turning purply-
black.
　　Culpepper says: 'an herbe of Saturne and an
anti-venerean, purges choleric humours, helps
sciatica and gout, and heals burns; it stays
bleedings.' Dried leaves acquire a pleasant
perfume; used as bookmarks in family Bibles.

BROOMRAPE, COMMON

Height 10–38cm/4–15in ✺ June–September

Orobanche minor
L *orobanche*, vetch-strangler

Parasitic on the roots of other plants,
all Broomrapes are devoid of chlorophyll.
Common Broomrape is unselective of its host,
and can therefore be seen alongside a variety
of plants. An unbranched stem, yellowy
brown tinged with red, bears pointed-oval
bracts and terminates with a cluster of orchid-
like yellowy-brown flowers, their lower lips
with 3 lobes, the upper a split hood. It
especially parasitises members of the pea
family, in particular clovers and vetches.
　　Medicinal or culinary uses unknown and
probably unlikely.

ANGELICA, WILD

KESH OR KESK (CUMBERLAND), GHOST KEX

Height 60–150cm/24–60in ❀ June–September

Angelica sylvestris
Med L *angelica*, angelic herb; L *sylvestris*,
woodland

A tall perennial of damp places with ridged,
hollow, purplish stems. Large divided leaves
with toothed leaflets have an inflated sheath
where they join the stem. Large umbrellas of
pinkish white flowers in globular clusters rise
on separate stems from large sheaths. Flattened
oval fruits have wings to aid dispersal.

The native British herb not as effective as
the cultivated species, but has been used as a
digestive herb for flatulence and stomach
conditions, and for clearing the eyes, ears and
teeth. Chewing the root was recommended
during the Plague of London in 1665. Like
Sweet Cicely, it sweetens sour fruits such as
gooseberries and rhubarb, although yielding
too much sugar to be safe for diabetics.

AVENS, MOUNTAIN

Height up to 8cm/3in ❀ April–June

Dryas octopetalla
Gk *dryades*, daughters of Zeus, oak nymphs;
L *octopetalla*, eight-petalled

A rare arctic alpine perennial under-shrub
whose creeping woody runners form low mats.
Hairy stalks with small clusters of evergreen,
oak-like basal leaves, dark green above, white
felted below, bear singly 8-petalled, white,
rose-like flowers up to an inch wide with a
central mass of golden stamens. Fruits are
nutlets, each with a long feathery parachute
combining to form a persistent clematis-like
plume.

Grows on high limestone turf or ledges.
Very rare in the Lake District, less so in
Snowdonia, but commoner in parts of
Upper Teesdale and Wharfedale.

BEDSTRAW, HEATH

ROCKSTRAW

Height 5–10cm, 2–4in ❀ June–August

Galium saxatile
Gk *gala*, milk; L *saxatilis*, rock
(growing among)

A short hairless perennial of acid grassland
with a loose mat of sprawling or ascending
flower stems. Its smooth, square stems are
much branched, and bear elliptical leaves
with forward-pointing marginal bristles in
whorls of 6–8. Clusters of small, white, sickly
scented flowers are borne on short stems.
The fruits are hairless and covered in small
warts. The flowers are larger than Limestone
Bedstraw (*Galium sterneri*), whose leaf margins
have backward-pointing bristles.

    Once used as a strewing herb to keep stone
floors sweet.

BEDSTRAW, HEDGE

Height 15–40cm/6–15in ❀ July–August

Galium mollugo
L *gala*, milk; *mollugo* from L *mollis*, soft, pliable

A scrambling hairless perennial with square,
smooth stems. Pale green, pointed, lance-
shaped, 1-veined leaves are arranged in
whorls of 6–8 up the stem. Branched loose
clusters of white flowers terminate the stems
and branches. Pairs of smooth globular fruits
turn black when ripe. Grows mainly in
hedgerows and verges.

    Like Lady's Bedstraw, it was once used for
dropsy, renal infections and stomach disorders.
It has been used as a useful source of dye, the
leaves producing a yellow hue, and the roots,
mixed with crowberry or cranberry fruits and
wood ash, yielding a beautiful scarlet.

BEDSTRAW, MARSH

Height 5–8cm/2–3in ❀ June–August

Galium palustre
L *gala*, milk; *palustre*, marsh

A straggly, hairless perennial with weak, square stems rough at the angles. Thin pointed leaves with rough edges are arranged in whorls of 4–6. Small clusters of white, 4-petalled flowers with very prominent dark red anthers (clearly seen with a hand lens) are held on short stems. Tiny seeds are black when ripe. Quite common, growing in or near water.

No known medicinal or culinary uses.

BISTORT, ALPINE

Height 10–20cm/4–8in ❀ June–August

Polygonum viviparum
Gk *poly*, many; *gony*, knee, L *viviparum*, germinating while still attached to its parent
Bistort from L *bis*, twice; *torta*, twisted (root)

A hairless perennial with an erect unbranched stem, bearing dark green lance-shaped leaves which taper towards the base like pointed paddles. Pinkish-white flowers cluster tightly up a slender upright spike. As they ripen the flowers are replaced from the bottom upwards by small purplish-red bulbils that can, if they do not drop off first, start to grow while still attached to the stem. A rare northern upland plant, more common in the Northern Pennines, especially in Upper Teesdale.

BLINKS

Height 2–5cm/1–2 in ❀ **April–October**

Montia fontana
After Giuseppi Monti (1682–1760), Italian
botanist; L *fontana*, of springs

An insignificant, sprawling, semi-aquatic
annual or perennial forming loose mats on
wet ground. Hairless branched stems, often
reddish, bear narrow, oval, opposite leaves.
Tiny white, short-stalked flowers borne
in small loose clusters at ends of stems
or branches. Seeds are tiny nuts. Common
on hillside flushes and mossy springs rising
through acid soils throughout the Lakes and
Dales. At lower levels it is often found on
or beside wet tracks, in muddy patches on
uncultivated land, and on the shores of lakes
and tarns. Sometimes grows submerged.

No known medicinal or culinary uses.

BOGBEAN

BUCKBEAN (YORKSHIRE, CUMBERLAND),
THREEFOLD (YORKSHIRE), MARSH TREFOIL

Height 20–32cm/8–13in ❀ **May–June**

Menyanthes trifoliata
Gk *menanthos*, moon flower; L *trifoliata*,
three-leaved

A hairless aquatic perennial with long, stout,
underwater runners. Upright stems rise above
the water surface bearing large trefoil leaves
on long stalks with a sheath at the base.
Spikes of up to 20 flowers rise on individual
stalks above the leaves. Each flower has 5
white starry petals fringed with white hairs;
the undersides of the petals are tinged pink.
Fruits are globular capsules crowned with
single styles.

Extracts from the leaves, occasionally the
whole plant, have been used against scurvy,
jaundice, rheumatism and fevers. The leaves
were used to flavour beer and to stimulate
appetite and digestion. It yields a green dye.

COTTON GRASS

BOG COTTON

Height 20–60cm/8–24in ❀ May–June

Eriophorum angustifolium
Gk *erion*, wool; L *phorum*, carrying; *angustus*,
narrow; *folium*, -leaved

Not a flower or a grass, but a perennial sedge
with a creeping rootstock that throws up
rooted stems at joints. The stems are round,
and bear long, slender, channelled leaves that
taper to a 3-sided point. The stems terminate
in a cluster of pale flowers with 3 stamens and
3 stigmas that develop long white hairs that
show as white balls. The fruits are clusters of
nutlets. Common in upland bogs and peat,
mostly on acid soils.

The fluffy heads were once used to make
wicks for candles, and to stuff pillows and
mattresses.

CRESS, THALE

Height 5–10cm/2–4in ❀ March–October

Arabidopsis thaliana
L *arabis*, genus of cresses; Gk *-opsis*,
resembling; *thaliana* after sixteenth-century
German botanist Johannes Thal, who first
recorded it

A fast-growing lightly hairy annual or
biennial of dry gritty places, often on waste
land, and well known as a garden weed. A
rosette of hairy toothed basal leaves supports
a stem with few unstalked untoothed leaves
that do not clasp the stem, and terminal
clusters of tiny white 4-petalled flowers that
develop stiff upright seed pods rising apart
from but parallel to the stem. Ripe pods burst
to scatter seeds if touched.

Grows throughout Europe and will seed
even in unpromising places such as tarmac.

GOOSEGRASS

CLEAVERS, SWEETHEARTS, STICKY WILLIE,
HAIROUGH OR HAYRIFT (YORKSHIRE)

Height 15–120cm/3–48in ❀ June–August

Galium aparine
Gk *gala*, milk; L *aparine*, goose

A scrambling brittle annual. Square, hairy,
adhesive stems are swollen at nodes bearing
whorls of 6 to 8 narrow hairy leaves with a
tiny bristle at tips. Insignificant 4-petalled
white flowers in stalked clusters. Globular
fruits covered in hooked bristles to aid
dispersal.

A purifier of the blood, helpful with skin
diseases and cancerous growths, head colds
and urinary conditions. Used for dropsy,
kidney and bladder disorders, piles and
stomach upsets. In Wensleydale still fed
to geese. Lowers blood pressure. Dioscorides
said stems were used by Greek shepherds to
strain hairs out of milk. It makes a shampoo
and hair tonic.

PARNASSUS, GRASS OF

Height 10–30cm/4–12in ❀ July–October

Parnassia palustris
Found in Oxfordshire in 1570 by Flemish
botanist Mathias de l'Obel who named it
Gramen parnassi in reference to Mount
Parnassus in Greece, which was associated
with Apollo and sacred to the muses;
L *palustris*, of marshes

Not a grass but an attractive perennial plant
with long-stalked, heart-shaped basal leaves
forming a loose rosette above an erect woody
stock. White, green-veined, 5-petalled flowers
are carried on individual stems clasped mid
way up by a single stalkless leaf. They smell
of honey. Fruit is a small capsule that splits
into 4 teeth to disperse seeds.

It was used in the first century AD to
dissolve kidney stones. Gerard called it White
Liverwort and used it for liver problems. It has
been used for centuries against diarrhoea, and
nervous and liver conditions.

PENNYWORT

NAVELWORT, KIDNEYWORT,
WALL PENNYROYAL

Height 10–40cm/4–16in   June–August

Umbilicus rupestris
L *umbilicus*, navel; *rupestris*, on rocks

A hairless fleshy perennial of walls, cliffs and
rocky outcrops. A rounded underground tuber
supports an open rosette of long-stalked,
toothed, round leaves with navel-like dimples
in their centres. A narrow unbranched
tapering spike of drooping bell-shaped
greenish-white flowers stands upright from
the base. Tiny brown seeds are crowded into
a pointed-oval seed case. Grows mainly in
South Lakeland, rare in Yorkshire Dales.

Once used for epilepsy, eye problems, piles,
burns and scalds. Culpeper recommended its
use for any inflammation, St Antony's Fire
(*Erysipelas*), gravel and kidney stones, piles,
gout and chilblains.

PENNYWORT, MARSH

SHEEP ROT (CUMBERLAND,
NORTHUMBERLAND), MARSH NAVELWORT

Height 5–10cm/2–4in   June–August

Hydrocotyle vulgaris
Gk *hydro*, water; L *cotyle*, cup-shaped;
vulgaris, common

A creeping, rooting perennial of damp acid
places. Erect hairy stalks bear round, slightly
lobed umbrella-shaped leaves with a central
dimple like Common Pennywort. Minute,
pinky-white flowers are borne in whorls on
separate stalks, often hidden by the leaves.
Insignificant but frequent in pools, ditches
and tarns in south and west Cumbria and
the eastern side of Eden Valley.

Culpepper says: 'It is under Venus, and is
good to break the stone and void it; also the
gravel in the reins or bladder.' As with Lesser
Spearwort, Butterwort and Sundew, it was
believed to cause foot rot and liver flukes in
sheep (endemic in their habitats).

PEPPER, WATER

ARSSMART, SMARTWEED

Height 25–75cm/10–30in ❀ July–October

Polygonum hydropiper
Gk *poly*, many; *gony*, knee; *hydro*, water;
piper, pepper

An erect hairless annual of shallow water or
damp places. Little-branched upright stems
bear narrow, pointed, lance-shaped leaves,
often wavy and fringed with hairs. Small
greenish-white or pinkish-white flowers are
borne on slender, nodding stems. Black seeds
are three-sided and nut-like. Common in
lowland streams and tarns.

 Biting and hot to the taste, the plant was
valued as an astringent, a diuretic, and a stem
to bleeding. Dioscorides used it for sores,
ulcers, swellings, toothache, jaundice, and
against fleas. The German name is *flohpfeffer*,
flea pepper.

SANDWORT, FINE-LEAVED

Height 5–10cm/2–4in ❀ May–September

Minuartia tenuifolia
After Juan Minuart (1693–1768) of
Barcelona; L *tenui*, thin; *folia*, leaved

A slender, much-branched, hairy annual.
An erect stem bears slim, linear, succulent-
looking leaves in stepped whorls rather like
Pearlwort. Loose clusters of 5-petalled white
flowers with slightly longer green, veined,
white edged sepals. Grows mainly on dry
stony ground, on chalk and limestone in
S England, but found on moist acid waste
land in the north. Particularly prolific on
Troutbeck Tongue (Walk 9).

SANDWORT, THREE-VEINED

THREE-NERVED SANDWORT

Height 15–30cm/6–12in ✿ May–July

Moehringia trinervia
After German botanist P. H. G. Möhring
(1710–1792); L *trinervia*, three-veined

A weak straggly annual of old woodland and
hedgerow. Superficially rather like chickweed
but with opposite pairs of pointed-oval leaves
with 3, sometimes 5 prominent veins on the
underside. Slim hairy stems bear solitary
white flowers with 5 undivided oval petals
half the size of its 5 hair-fringed sepals.
Rounded fruit splits to release oily brown
seeds that attract ants which disperse them.
Common on lighter lowland and woodland
soils.
Medicinal or culinary uses obscure.

SAXIFRAGE, MOSSY

DOVEDALE MOSS

Height 5–15cm/2–6in ✿ May–July

Saxifraga hypnoides
L *saxum*, rock; *frangere*, to break;
Gk *hyp-*, below; *noides*, nodes

A mat-forming perennial with long, slender,
leafy and hairy shoots. Lower leaves are
alternate and divided into 3–7 narrow fingers,
while the upper leaves are usually single
spears. Erect, branched flowering stems bear
few 5-petalled flowers with pink tips that
nod in bud. First recorded in Lancashire
by Parkinson in 1640, it grows up to high
altitudes on limy or acid soils. Cultivated
as a popular rockery or edging plant.

SAXIFRAGE, STARRY

Height 5–25cm/2–10in ❀ June–August

Saxifraga stellaris
L *saxum*, rock; *frangere*, to break; *stellaris*, starry

A low, slightly hairy perennial with a dense rosette of unstalked toothed leaves. A pinkish erect stem carries a loose cluster of star-like, 5-petalled white flowers, each petal having 2 yellow spots at the base, and bearing prominent red anthers. The sepals turn down. Discovered on Snowdon in 1639 by Thomas Johnson. A widespread upland plant of springs, gullies or streams.

It was once used to break kidney and bladder stones. Its roots steeped in vinegar were recommended against the plague.

SCURVYGRASS

SCROOBY GRASS (NORTHERN ENGLAND), SPOONWORT (FROM LEAF SHAPE)

Height 10–50cm/4–20in ❀ May–August

Cochlearia officinalis
L *cochlearia*, spoon-shaped, from Gk *kochlos*, snail shell; L *officinalis*, of the apothecary

A fleshy perennial with a long taproot. Basal rosettes of sprawling long-stalked, untoothed kidney-shaped succulent leaves. Smooth stems bear clasping, unstalked, slightly toothed leaves, and loose spikes of small white 4-petalled flowers. Globular seed pods.

Gerard gives the symptoms of scurvy: 'the gums are loosed, swolne, and exulcerate; the mouth greevously stinking; the thighs and legs are withal verie often full of blewe spots, not much unlike those that come of bruses; the face and the rest of the bodie is often times of a pale colour; and the feete are swolne as in the dropsy.' The plant was used as a salad or a drink, and carried on ships against scurvy.

SNEEZEWORT

BACHELORS' BUTTONS

Height 30–60cm/12–24in   ❀ July–August

Achillea ptarmica
After Achilles, who used it medicinally;
Gk *ptarmika*, to sneeze

A hairy perennial with a woody creeping
rootstock. Hairy, angular, erect stems bear
unstalked, sharply lance-shaped leaves with
fine teeth on the margins. Small white-rayed
daisy-like flowers are borne in loose, branched
clusters, the unrayed central florets greenish-
white. Seeds blackish. Grows in damp, grassy
places on acid or neutral soils.

Found in Kentish Town by John Gerard,
who said its smell was enough to make one
sneeze. Its hot, biting leaves were used to spice
up salads. The roots held in the mouth taste
sharp, cause saliva to flow, and ease toothache.

STITCHWORT, LESSER

Height 30–90cm/12–36in   ❀ June–August

Stellaria graminae
L *stellaria*, star-like; *gramineus*, grass-like

A creeping perennial with fragile many-
branched, smooth, square stems. Smooth,
narrow pointed lance-shaped leaves are borne
in opposite pairs, often with small pointed
bracts at their bases. Loose clusters of 5-
petalled white flowers are carried on slender,
branching stems. The petals are deeply cleft
to the base and are the same length as the
slim green sepals. It grows on poor soils,
sometimes tolerating damp conditions,
throughout the region.

Gerard used it to cure the stitch, or pain
in the side, but found it less effective than
Greater Stitchwort.

STITCHWORT, MARSH

Height 5–10cm/2–4in   🌸 June–August

Stellaria palustris
L *stellaria*, little star; *palustris*, of swampy places

A creeping greyish perennial with upright
smooth square stems with opposite pairs
of narrow waxy grey lance-shaped leaves.
Slender-stalked 5-petalled white flowers
are borne in loose clusters. The 5 petals are
deeply cleft, the 5 slim green sepals half the
length of the petals. The seeds are in globular
capsules.

Becoming rare in Cumbria and the
Yorkshire Dales, possibly through loss of
habitats. It is often supplanted by the more
common but smaller Bog Stitchwort (*Stellaria
uliginosa*), which has smaller flowers, rather
like Chickweed with green-veined sepals
much longer than the petals.

Any medicinal or culinary uses obscure.

STITCHWORT, WOOD

WOOD CHICKWEED

Height 30–60cm/12–24in   🌸 May–July

Stellaria nemorum
L *stellaria*, starry; *nemorum*, of woods

A hairy perennial rising from an underground
stolon. Round hairy stems bear opposite pairs
of pointed oval leaves, lower ones stalked,
upper narrower and unstalked. 5 deeply cleft
white petals are almost twice as long as the
hairless sepals. Common in moist woodlands
or by stream-sides on acid soils. Proliferates
inter alia in Strid Wood, Wharfedale and
near Aysgarth Mill Race in Wensleydale.

It was taken in wine to ease stitch in the
side, as its English common name suggests.
Other medicinal properties questionable.

STONECROP, ENGLISH

Height up to 5cm/2in   ❀ June–August

Sedum anglicum
L *sedere*, to sit; *anglicum*, English

A low, loose, mat-forming perennial with creeping stems that root frequently at intervals. It has alternate, cylindrical-oval fleshy leaves tinged red when young. Pointed 5-petalled white flowers with prominent black anthers, pink below, are borne in small clusters atop short stems. Seeds in a multiple capsule like a small cluster of bulbils. Flowers similar to yellow Wall Pepper.

Herbalists used this plant, but preferred Biting Stonecrop (*Sedum acre*), as a vermifuge, for scrofula, fevers and dropsy. Also used for piles and to remove warts and corns.

SUNDEW

ROUND-LEAVED SUNDEW, YOUTHGRASS, YOUTHWORT

Height 5–27cm/2–11in   ❀ June–August

Drosera rotundifolia
Gk *droseros*, dewy; L *rotundifolia*, round-leaved

A tiny insectivorous perennial usually growing on sphagnum moss. A rosette of long-stalked, round, yellow-green leaves covered with short glandular hairs, each tipped with a globule of sticky fluid. Erect, hairy, unbranched stems bear white 5-petalled flowers with green sepals. The fruit is a many-sided capsule. Growing on acid moorland lacking in nutrients, it extracts essential minerals from trapped flies.

The 'dew' was once considered to have magical properties as a charm to entrap lovers and an aphrodisiac for cattle. It was used for whooping cough, consumption and asthma. Its juice was said to remove warts and corns. Its caustic leaves cause liver-rot in sheep.

49

SUNDEW, OBLONG-LEAVED

LONG-LEAVED SUNDEW

Height 5–27cm/2–11in ❀ June–August

Drosera intermedia
Gk *droseros*, dewy; L *intermedia*, middle-sized

A low insectivorous plant similar to Common
or Round-leaved Sundew, growing in small
rosettes on mounds of sphagnum moss. Narrow
oblong leaves resemble canoe paddles on long
hairless stalks with characteristic red hairs
and sticky droplets or 'dew'. Small white 5-
petalled flowers are borne on stout, hairless,
arching stalks rising from the side of the rosette.
It is very rare, found only in the Lake District,
W Ireland and NW Scotland. In the Lakes it is
found on the wet edges of pools in the Furness
fells and the Solway mosses. It may be seen in
the boggy hollow between Beacon Fell and
Fisher High, growing alongside Common
Sundew (Walk 1).

   Folk lore and medicinal uses the same as for
Common Sundew.

YARROW

MILFOIL, OLD MAN'S BACCY
(NORTHUMBERLAND), SOLDIERS'
WOUNDWORT, NOSE-BLEED

Height up to 60cm/24in ❀ June–September

Achillea millefolium
After Achilles who used it to stem the
bleeding from his soldiers' wounds;
L *millefolium*, thousand leaflets
AS *gearwe*, yarrow

An erect hairy perennial with a rough angular
stem branching at the top and bearing long
alternate bi-pinnate (feathery) leaves. White
flowers, often with a lilac tint, like small
daisies are held in loose terminal heads.
Tiny seeds are winged.

   Has had many uses, against colds and
fevers, bleeding piles and kidney disorders,
to purify the blood and arrest hair loss. Some
Scots shepherds thought it good against sheep
scab. Swedes used it to flavour beer.

BURDOCK, LESSER

BURDOCKEN (YORKSHIRE), CLOUTS (N ENGLAND)

Height 60–120cm/24–48in ❀ July–September

Arctium minus
Gk *arktos*, bear (shaggy hair); L *minus*, lesser

A tall biennial of woods and waysides, with
a hairy, reddish, erect, stem and drooping
branches. At the base it has large, pointed
oval, hollow-stalked leaves up to 50cm/20in
long, and alternate, narrower upper leaves
with stalks and blades of equal length, about
30cm/12in. Purple, globular, thistle-like
flowers up to 2cm/1in across are borne in
loose terminal spikes. The bracts of the flower
cups and the purple florets are tipped with
stout spines to cling to animals.

Gerard prescribed young shoots as an
aphrodisiac. Leaves were applied to sores and
wounds, the juice to soothe burns and bites.
Seeds used for sciatica; gipsies wore them in
a bag round the neck against rheumatism.
Burdock Oil promotes hair growth.

BURNET, GREAT

RED HEADS (YORKSHIRE), DRUMSTICKS
(SOUTHWEST ENGLAND)

Height 30–90cm/12–36in ❀ June–September

Sanguisorbia officinalis
L *sanguis*, blood; *sorbeo*, staunch;
officinalis, medicinal herb
Burnet from brunette, dark reddish-brown

A perennial plant with a woody stock and
upright hairless branched stems bearing
distinctive pinnate leaves made up of 3–7
opposite pairs of short-stalked, toothed leaflets
and a similar terminal leaflet. When crushed
they smell of cucumbers. Flowers are borne,
male and female separately, in dense terminal
clusters. The lower male flowers are greenish,
with reddish-purple female flowers above
them. 4 sepals, 4 stamens, but no petals.
Fruits are tiny 4-winged nutlets.

Staunches bleeding, eases diarrhoea and
intestinal disorders. Young leaves and shoots
used in spring salads, soups and as vegetables.

51

CINQUEFOIL, MARSH

BOG STRAWBERRY

Height 15–45cm/6–18in ❀ May–July

Potentilla palustris
L *potens*, powerful (medicinally); *palustris*,
of marshes
Fr *cinque*, five; *foil*, leaved

A northern marshland perennial with a
creeping underground stem. Hairy, upright
stems bear alternately, toothed, hairy,
5-fingered green leaves. Slender, hairy,
redddish stems bear loose clusters of reddish-
purple 5-petalled starry flowers whose pointed
oval sepals are much larger than the slim
pointed petals. Many seeds are carried in
a spongy cup enclosed by the sepals. Grows
in marshes, mosses and boggy pools, mostly
at lower levels, throughout the region.

No recorded medicinal use, but possibly
used instead of Creeping Cinquefoil as an
astringent and febrifuge.

FOXGLOVE

THIMBLES (CUMBERLAND), LADY'S THIMBLE,
FAIRIES' THIMBLES

Height 60–150cm/24–60in ❀ June–August

Digitalis purpurea
L *digitus*, finger; *purpurea*, purple
OE *foxes glofa*, glove of the fox or folks (fairies)

Erect, sometimes branching biennial or
perennial. In year 1 produces a spreading
rosette of large toothed, wrinkled leaves up to
30cm/12in long. In year 2 a flower stem rises
with similar but short wing-stalked leaves
diminishing upwards. At the top is a spike of
purple tubular flowers, spotted inside, all on
the same side of the stem. Seeds are in ovate
capsules.

A most important drug from its leaf extracts,
digitoxin and gitoxin for heart disorders. Once
used as a purge, for fevers and against dropsy
and scrofula. Leaves put in children's shoes for
a year cured scarlet fever. European counterpart
Digitalis lanata used for drug extraction.

HEATHER, BELL

CARLIN HEATHER (CARLIN MEANING WITCH
OR HAG)

Height 20–60cm/8–24in ❀ July–September

Erica cinerea
Gk *eireke*, classical name for Heath family;
L *cinerea*, grey

An evergreen shrub that grows on the drier
tussocks of damp acid moorlands. Woody
branches bear green twigs, hairy at first,
bearing short needle-like greyish leaves in
whorls of three with their edges rolled down.
To preserve moisture, the leaves have a thick
cuticle or protective surface layer. Crimson-
purple egg- or bell-shaped flowers have very
short sepals and hang like bells. A rich
honey-bearing plant much favoured by bees.
The flowering tips, eaten by grouse, were once
used to treat snake bites. Now, with its many
cultivars, a very popular garden plant.

KNAPWEED

HARDHEADS (YORKSHIRE, CUMBERLAND),
HORSEKNOPS, PAINTBRUSH

Height 30–60cm/12–24in ❀ June–September

Centaurea nigra
After Chiron, wisest of the Centaurs who used
it to heal wounds; L *nigra*, black (patterning on
calyx)

A downy perennial with stiff ribbed stems.
Lower leaves are lance-shaped with short teeth
and long stalks, upper leaves neither toothed
nor stalked. Solitary or small clusters of
crowded purple flowers in a globular, thistle-
like cup with blackish, bristly bracts held erect
at stem tops. Seeds have short hairs on top.
Lives in coarse grass and roadsides.

   Used for wounds, ruptures, bruises, scabs,
sore throats, and for rubbing on cows' udders
after calving. Maidens foretold their marriage
prospects by pulling off the outer florets and
placing the rest of the flower in their blouse.

LING

HEATHER

Height 15–60cm/6–24in ✤ **August–September**

Calluna vulgaris
L *kalluno*, to cleanse or brush; L *vulgaris*,
common
Ling from AS *lig*, fire (used as a fuel)

A short, woody, evergreen plant of acid heath,
moor and bog. Unstalked, scaled, overlapping
and congested opposite leaves extend from
woody stems. Loose branched spikes of purple
flowers at tops of stems have large sepals that
obscure the petals behind. Common in both
dry moors and wet mosses, but may be found
on leached soil in limestone areas. Grouse
and sheep graze on young shoots and seeds.
Nectar-rich flowers attract bees.

    Used historically for bedding, besoms,
thatch, fuel, baskets, rope, fodder and orange
dye. Heather ale brewed by the Bronze Age
Picts. The family badge of the MacDonnels.

LOBELIA, WATER

WATER GLADIOLE (CUMBERLAND)

Height 15–20cm/6–8in ✤ **July–August**

Lobelia dortmanna
Lobelia after Flemish botanist Mathias de
l'Obel (1538–1616); Dortmanna after
Dortmann, c. 1640

A hairless aquatic perennial with submerged
rosettes of untoothed, hollow, linear leaves
rising from a stolon in the bottom mud.
Hollow flower stems with a few small bracts
rise above the surface to bear a few loose,
drooping, lilac-coloured flowers, tubular with
3 hanging and 2 upright petals, similar to
the garden Lobelia. Found in acid lakes, pools
and reservoirs. A northern plant, located
mainly in S and W Cumbria, e.g. Angle Tarn,
Beacon Tarn and Torver Tarn.

    Little used medicinally, but has helped
both headaches and noises in the ears.

ORCHID, NORTHERN MARSH

DWARF PURPLE ORCHID, CAIN AND ABEL

Height 10–25cm/4–10in ❀ June–July

Orchis purpurella
Gk *orchis*, testicle (from tubers' shape);
L *purpurella*, little purple

The smallest of the marsh orchids, with tubers
divided into 2–4 spreading lobes. A stout
aerial stem has 4–9 dark green lance-shaped
leaves towards the base, with a few small spots
near hooded tips. The erect flower spikes vary
from 2.5–10cm/1–4 in long, and bear large,
brilliant red-purple flowers with an untoothed
flat lip and irregular broken-line markings,
and a thick spur. A northern and western
counterpart of the Heath Spotted Orchid.
Rare in upland Lakeland, but common up the
Eden Valley. Prolific patches found on North
Walney Island.

The roots hold a starchy substance called
bassorin that was made into salep, a hot drink.
Also used for diarrhoea and biliousness.

PANSY, MOUNTAIN

Height 7.5–20cm/3–8in ❀ May–August

Viola lutea
L *viola*, plant's name; *lutea*, yellow
Pansy from Fr *pensée*, thought

An almost hairless perennial with creeping
underground stems from which aerial stalks
rise at intervals. Toothed, oval leaves have
small leaf-like stipules near the stem joint,
from the uppermost of which rise slender,
upright flower stems bearing single, rarely up
to 4, flat-faced flowers. These may be yellow,
purple or bi-coloured, and have 4 erect petals,
and a larger pendant petal, often marked with
dark guide lines. Seeds are held in a capsule
that splits into 3 for dispersal. Used to breed
garden pansies.

Flowers yellow in Yorkshire and Derbyshire;
purple and yellow-purple in Teesdale and
Scotland. Grows at around 300m/1,000ft
in N England and Scotland; most prolific in
N Yorkshire, Eden Valley and north Lakeland.

ROSEMARY, BOG

Height 5–25cm/2–10in ❀ May–June

Andromeda polifolia
Andromeda after an Ethiopian princess, who
was chained to a cliff to appease a monster
and saved by Perseus; L *polifolia*, grey-leaved

An evergreen sub-shrub with spreading root
stems and erect flowering stems. Elliptical
leaves, grey-green above and white below,
have margins rolled down. Terminal loose
clusters of nodding, bell-shaped, pink flowers
on relatively long stalks which develop into
greyish seed capsules. A very rare plant that
grows mainly on sphagnum mosses which,
due to agricultural and forestry drainage, is
becoming scarcer. Commonest in the raised
bogs of S and N Cumbria but also occurs in
wet acid habitats over most of Europe.

SPEEDWELL, HEATH

COMMON SPEEDWELL

Height 10–30cm/4–12in ❀ May–August

Veronica officinalis
After St Veronica who wiped Christ's face
on his way to the cross; L *officinalis*, of the
monastic herb store

A perennial with creeping, rooting stems.
Erect hairy stems bear hairy, opposite,
toothed, short-stalked ovallish leaves. The
flowering spikes are made up of ascending
pairs of veined, lilac flowers, each with 4
petals of unequal sizes. Seeds are in heart-
shaped capsules. Commonly found throughout
the area on well-drained, neutral soils.

Astringent and bitter. Only recently
superseded by synthetic drugs in orthodox
medicine and still used extensively in
homeopathy for skin ailments, stomach upsets,
rheumatism, and in herbal teas. Once also
used for wounds, coughs, fevers, consumption
and kidney stones.

THISTLE, CREEPING

WAY THISTLE, CREEPING PLUME THISTLE

Height 30–150cm/12–60in ❀ June–September

Cirsium arvense
L *cirsium*, of the thistle family; *arvense*,
of cultivated ground
OE *thistel*, to prick

A hairless perennial with a white, creeping,
branching rootstock that creates spreading
clumps. Spineless, upright branched stems
bear short-stalked, spiny, lobed leaves, hairless
above, often downy beneath. Upper leaves are
unstalked. Pale purple thistle flowerheads held
upright on slender stems either singly, or in
loose groups of 2–5, held by tulip-shaped cups
bearing pointed, purple-tipped bracts. Seeds
like tiny shuttlecocks are wind dispersed.
Pestilential weeds, Creeping Thistles grow
on rich, but neglected farmland.

   The seeds can provide useful oils, but are
not exploited. After crushing to destroy the
prickles, the plant can be fed to animals.

THISTLE, MARSH

MARSH PLUME THISTLE

Height 60–180cm/24–72in ❀ June–September

Cirsium palustre
L *Cirsium*, of the thistle family; L *palustre*,
marsh

A tall hairy perennial, the stems winged to
the top with spines. Narrow spiny unstalked
leaves are hairy on the upper sides. Slender
spiny stems branch from leaf axils to bear up
to 8 upright, purple flowerheads with narrow-
headed green cups covered with purple-tinged
pointed bracts. It can also have white flowers.
The seeds have parachutes of fine hairs. Very
common.

   Culpeper said the stalks were, like those of
the Milk Thistle (*Silybum marianum*), effective
with fevers, jaundice, dropsy and kidney
stones. He recommended the young shoots,
prickles removed, to be boiled and eaten as a
spring blood-cleanser. Gerard vouched it the
best cure for melancholy.

THISTLE, SPEAR

BUR THISTLE

Height 30–150cm/12–60in ❀ July–October

Cirsium vulgare
L *cirsium*, family of thistles; *vulgare*, common

A tall biennial with sharp, spiny wings right up to the top of its sturdy stem. Dull green, spiny, deeply cut, lance-shaped leaves with rough prickles on the upper side join the stem with long, spiny wings. The undersides are almost white with a cover of softer hairs. 1–3 flowers in a bristly globular hedgehog covered with narrow spiky yellow bracts topped by a reddish-purple plume, can be up to 2.5cm/1in across and 5cm/2in high. Seeds have a feathery shuttlecock to aid dispersal.

Closely related to the Creeping Thistle, it has the same properties and uses. Children used to peel off the bracts on the flower head and eat the nutty core.

TOADFLAX, IVY-LEAVED

THE MADONNA'S FLOWER

Height 10–76cm/4–30in ❀ May–October

Cymbalaria muralis
Gk *kymbalon*, cymbal (dimpled leaf);
L *muralis*, of walls

A hairless, tumbling perennial seen mainly on walls or buildings up to about 450m/1,475ft. Frequently rooting clinging stems bear ivy-like leaves alternately; long fine stalks raise flowers like snapdragons above the leaves. They have lilac hoods and spurs and yellow lower lips. Globular fruit cases curve down to deposit ridged seeds close to germination points. A Mediterranean plant introduced in London in mid-seventeenth century as a rockery plant; it escaped and naturalised prolifically, preferring limy soil or mortar, but it can grow even in bricks.

Has anti-scorbutic powers and is eaten in S Europe as a salad plant. Yields a yellow dye.

VIOLET, MARSH

BOG VIOLET

Height 5–10cm/2–4in ❀ April–July

Viola palustris
Viola, plant's name; *palustris*, marsh

A short, hairless perennial with a creeping underground stolon. Long-stalked, lightly toothed, almost round kidney-shaped leaves rise individually from the base (the leaves of Dog Violet have no stems and are pointed). Solitary, long-stalked, pale lilac flowers also rise from the roots, veined dark purple and with a short blunt spur. Each flower stem bears a pair of small leaf-like bracts part way up. Seeds in a hairless capsule. Unlike some plants of this genus, Marsh Violet is unscented. Grows in acid bogs and woods in N Britain, often with sphagnum moss. Common in acid uplands, lowland marshes and willow carr.

No known medicinal uses.

WILLOWHERB, ROSE BAY

FIREWEED, BLOOMING SALLY (SALIX, WILLOW)

Height 60–150cm/24–60in ❀ June–September

Chamaenerion angustifolium
Gk *chamae*, on the ground; *nerion*, Oleander or Rose Bay; L *angusti*, narrow; *folium*, leaved

A sturdy, hairless perennial rising from thick, spreading, woody roots. Erect, unbranched stems bear spirally alternate, narrow lance-like leaves with wavy, slightly toothed edges like willow. Pinky-purple flowers with 4 slightly notched petals and 4 dark purple sepals borne in long tapering spikes. A long, slim, 4-sided capsule below each flower splits when ripe to release plumed seeds.

Used against stomach complaints and skin problems. Linnaeus said the leaves and young shoots could be used as vegetables. In Britain the leaves were made into an astringent tea. Still used in Russia to make kaporie tea and, with Fly Agaric fungus, a potent drink.

WOUNDWORT, MARSH

CLOWN'S WOUNDWORT, ALL HEAL

Height 40–100cm/16–40in ❋ July–September

Stachys palustris
Gk *stachys*, spike; L *palustris*, marsh

A hairy perennial with stout, spreading, fleshy, underground stolons which throw up erect, 4-sided flower stems bearing short-stalked, hairy, toothed, lance-shaped leaves in opposite pairs. Whorls of pale purple, dark purple-spotted, snapdragon-like flowers are spaced above small unstalked leaves up the spike.

Gerard relates how he met a labourer with a scythe wound to the leg, right down to the bone. Refusing Gerard's help, he dressed the bleeding wound himself with leaves of this plant, and within a week it was healed; Gerard named it Clownwort. Used to relieve gout, cramp and vertigo. Young shoots can be eaten as asparagus, as also the tubers collected in autumn.

BARTSIA, ALPINE

Height 7.5–15cm/3–6in ☘ July–August

Bartsia alpina
Named by Linnaeus after his friend
Dr Bartoch, a Dutch physician; L *alpina*,
of high uplands

A downy, semi-parasitic perennial reminiscent
of Yellow Rattle or Lousewort. Unstalked,
purple, hairy, oval leaves are arranged in
opposite pairs up a short hairy reddish stem.
Opposite pairs of deep purple snap-dragon-
like flowers nestle above leaf joints to form a
crowded spike. The flowers are open, 2-lipped,
and also very hairy. Seeds in a capsule longer
than the calyx. Grows in damp, lime-rich
grassland. Very rare but often seen in Upper
Teesdale, especially on river banks near
Widdybank Farm.
 No known medicinal use, but Red Bartsia
once used as a toothache cure.

BILBERRY

BLAEBERRY (NORTHERN ENGLAND, SCOTLAND),
WHINBERRY OR BLUEBERRY (N ENGLAND)

Height 22–45cm/9–18in ☘ April–June

Vaccinium myrtilis
L *Vaccinium*, name used by Pliny; *myrtilis*,
a small myrtle

A hairless deciduous, creeping shrub with
numerous ascending green stems. 3-angled
green twigs bear bright green, toothed, pointed-
oval leathery leaves that turn red in autumn.
Globular, waxy, pink flowers hang singly or
in pairs like little lanterns with a small frill.
The round fruits turn bluish-black when ripe.
Common on uplands, lowland heaths and
mosses, and acid birch/oak woods.
 First recorded as a medicine by Hildegard
of Bingen. Ripe berries are mildly laxative, but
dried ones binding and antibacterial, therefore
good for diarrhoea and dysentery. Used for
scurvy, urinary complaints and diabetes. Fruits
eaten in tarts, jellies or jam, or raw with cream.

BINDWEED, FIELD

BINDWEED, BELLBINE, CORNBINE,
DEVIL'S GUTS

Height 20–76cm/8–30in ❀ June–September

Convolvulus arvensis
L *convolvere*, to twine; *arvensis*, of cultivated
ground

An invasive perennial weed of cultivation
and waste ground. Extensive often deep white
roots throw up scrambling or twining stems
of up to 60cm/24in long that strangle other
plants for support. Alternate arrow-shaped
leaves on slim stalks. Pink or white funnel-
shaped flowers with white stripes above and
wide mauve stripes below smell sweetly of
almonds. Globular fruit has 2–4 seeds.
Common in the lowlands on the Lakeland
fringe, less so except for small colonies in
North Yorkshire.

A strong purgative, its flowers give a rich
orange or yellow tint to water that is deepened
by the addition of alum and alkalies.

BUTTERBUR

WILD RHUBARB, CLOUTS (BOTH N ENGLAND),
PLAGUEWORT (CORNWALL)

Height 15–45cm/6–18in ❀ March–May

Petasites hybridus
Gk *petasus*, hat (leaves); L *hybridis*, hybrid

A perennial with stout creeping tubers that
often form large patches. Stout, hollow upright
stems rise before the leaves with green lance-
shaped scales and broad spikes of pink, short-
stalked unrayed flowers in broad green cups.
Male and female flowers on separate spikes,
the male being taller and slimmer. Long-
stalked, toothed, heart-shaped, rhubarb-like
leaves develop later, green above, silky below.

The roots, dried and powdered and mixed
with wine, were used to promote perspiration
against fevers and plague, to help wheeziness
and to kill worms. Leaves were used for
poulticing flesh wounds and skin complaints,
and in the North for wrapping butter.

COWBERRY

RED WHORTLEBERRY

Height up to 15cm/6in ❀ May–June

Vaccinium vitis-idaea
L *Vaccinium*, name used by Pliny; *vitis*, grape;
idaea, from Mount Ida

A creeping evergreen sub shrub of acid moors.
Round, downy twigs support alternate dark
green leathery leaves, oval with notched tips
and the edges rolled back. Pink, bell-shaped
flowers with a pointed frill at the bottom
hang in drooping clusters from the tops of the
stems. Fruits are tart red berries, much eaten
by sheep and grouse.

A urinary antiseptic, also helpful for
cystitis. Decoctions are taken for arthritis,
rheumatic conditions, diabetes and diarrhoea,
but arbutin content renders prolonged use
unsafe. The red berries make an excellent
jelly. Leaves and stems yield a yellow dye.
The family badge of the McLeods.

CRANBERRY

CRANEBERRY, MARSH WHORTLEBERRY

Height 15cm/6in ❀ May–June

Vaccinium oxycoccus
Vaccinium, name used by Pliny; Gk *oxys*, acid;
kokkus, round berry

A straggly evergreen subshrub that colonises
sphagnum moss hummocks. Its slender,
prostrate, rooting stems bear alternate oval
untoothed leaves, dark green above, silvery
below. Upright, thread-like reddish stems bear
up to 4 bright pink lantern-like flowers with
4 curled-back petals and prominent pink
and yellow stamens. Fruits are round or pear-
shaped edible berries. Trailing stems up to
30cm/12 in long. Grows in upland bogs or
in damp pine or birch woods.

Until the introduction of larger American
species these berries were widely used for jam,
pie-filling, and as a sauce for venison or wild
fowl. Queen Victoria enjoyed 'a good tart of
cranberries' when at Balmoral.

CROWBERRY

CROW PEA (USA)

Height 15–45cm/6–18in ❀ April–May

Empetrum nigrum
Gk *en*, on; *petron*, rock; L *nigrum*, black
Crowberry because it is fit only for crows
to eat or because of its colour

A creeping, evergreen, mat-forming perennial
shrub. Slender, sprawling twigs, reddish when
young, support spiralling, shiny, incurved
leaves (top). Minute pink flowers spring
from leaf joints, the male flowers with 3 long
stamens, the slightly larger female flowers on
separate plants with a crown-like cluster of
6–9 stiles (below). The fruit is a tasteless berry
– first green, then pink, then shiny black–
eaten by most moor birds. The leaves support
the caterpillars of several moths, including
Mountain Burnet. Common on upland moors
or on lower mosses under birch scrub.

Boiled in alum water, berries can be used
to dye yarn black.

HEATH, CROSS-LEAVED

BOG HEATHER, FATHER OF HEATH (YORKSHIRE)

Height 20–60cm/8–24in ❀ July–September

Erica tetralix
Gk *ereike*, heather; *tetra*, 4 (leaves in a whorl)

A greyish evergreen sub shrub with thin,
hairy, down-curved, needle-like leaves
arranged in whorls of 4 forming crosses up
the stems. The leaves are paler underneath.
At the tops of the stems are tight clusters of
drooping, globular, pink, lantern-like flowers.
Their fruits are downy. A common plant
of wet moors, bogs and mosses on acid soils.
Flowers are similar to Bell Heather, which
grows in drier positions. In Cumbria it
occurs in raised peatlands along with
sphagnum mosses and Cotton Grasses up
to 600m/1970ft, but in the Yorkshire Dales
it does not occur below 250m/820ft.

LOUSEWORT

BEE SOUKIES, DWARF RED RATTLE

Height 5–10cm/2–4in   ❀ April–July

Pedicularis sylvatica
L *pediculus*, louse (reputed to deter); *sylvatica*,
woods, or growing wild

A semi-parasitic perennial that extracts
moisture and minerals from neighbouring
grass roots. Hairless, unbranched, ascending
stems bear alternate, stalked, toothed, Burnet-
like leaves, i.e. with opposite pairs and one
terminal leaflet. Comparatively large, pink,
snapdragon-like flowers with blunt upper
hoods and 3-lobed lips crowd up a short leafy
spike. A green tubular cup that inflates when
the seeds are ripe cradles each flower. Not
uncommon in acid bogs and wet moorland.

   In medieval times it was thought that
animals grazing on it became infested with
lice, as well as developing flukeworms.

LOUSEWORT, MARSH

RED RATTLE

Height 7.5–30cm/3–12in   ❀ May–September

Pedicularis palustris
L *pediculus*, louse; *palustris*, marsh

A semi-parasitic biennial whose roots attach
to adjacent plants, usually grasses, for water
and mineral salts. A single, branched, upright
purplish stem bears usually alternate, deeply
divided leaves rather like fern fronds. Short-
stalked, veined, pink snapdragon-like flowers
rise from leaf joints to form a loose spike,
their 2-lipped cups expanding around the
ripening seeds, that can be heard to rattle
when shaken. Rarer than Lousewort, but
found, usually in long grass, in marshy fields
or beside tarns.

   A styptic and a wound herb. Culpeper said
that, boiled in port, it was 'profitable to heal
fistulas and hollow ulcers and to stay the flux
of humours in them, as also the abundance of
the courses or any other flux of blood'.

ORCHID, HEATH SPOTTED

DEAD MEN'S FINGERS

Height 10–38cm/4–15in ❀ June–August

Dactyllorhiza maculata
Gk *dactylos*, finger; L *rhiza*, root; *maculata*,
spotted

The first leaf is produced in the second year
after germination, developing over several
more years before flowering. Its small tubers
often multiply to form clumps of aerial shoots.
4–8 narrow, keeled, lance-shaped leaves,
usually spotted purplish-black, clasp the stem.
Flowers held in a short cylindrical spike, fewer
but larger than Spotted Orchids, with a broad
lip of 2 large lobes and a small pointed one in
the centre. Its slender spur is as long as the
lip. Grows in damp, acid moors, mosses and
upland meadows (the Common Spotted
Orchid grows in limy soils).

Tubers once used, as with other orchids,
to make salep.

ORPINE

MIDSUMMER MEN (NORTHUMBERLAND),
LIVELONG

Height 20–60cm/8–24in ❀ July–September

Sedum telephium
L *sedere*, to sit; Gk *telephium*, plant's name
OF *orpiment*, a golden pigment

A greyish perennial with tuberous roots. Pale
green stems, often with a reddish tinge, bear
alternate, flat, toothed, succulent leaves. The
head of the stem holds dense, round-topped
clusters of reddish, 5-petalled, star-like flowers
on short reddish stalks. It is like a straggly
garden Ice Plant (*Sedum spectabile*).

The leaves, eaten with other salad herbs,
were considered beneficial for fevers, female
sterility and excessive menstrual flow.
The roots were used for scrofula. Culpeper
recommended it for cancer, and it was used
by Napoleon who died of the disease. It was
believed to have magical powers, to foretell
the future and to dispel evil.

PARSLEY, HEDGE

UPRIGHT HEDGE PARSLEY, LACE FLOWER,
DEVIL'S NIGHTCAP, SCABBY HEAD

Height 5–90cm/2–36in ❀ July–September

Torilis japonica
Gk *torilis*, engraved (fruits); L *japonica*,
Japanese (i.e. Asiatic)

A tall, hairy annual, one of the last
umbellifers to flower. Its stiff upright stems
are solid and ridged and the leaves alternate,
coarsely toothed, 1- to 3-pinnate (fern-like,
reminiscent of Cow Parsley, *Anthriscus
sylvestris*). Pink flowers are borne on straight,
spreading, slender stalks in small loose balls
that make up a delicate larger globular cluster.
The egg-shaped fruits are covered with
curved, hooked spines. A common plant
of dry hedgerows, scrubland, woodland edges
and grassy pastures.

PIMPERNEL, BOG

Height 5–15cm/2–6in ❀ June–August

Anagalis tenella
Gk *anagalis*, delightful (named by
Dioscorides); L *tenella*, dainty
Pimpernel from *bipinella*, little 2-winged
(2-leaved) flower

A slender, creeping perennial of wet places.
Sprawling slim stems that root frequently bear
opposite pairs of pointed-oval leaves, paler
than those of the Scarlet Pimpernel. Pale
pink waxy flowers rise on long fine stalks
along the stems. The fruits are borne singly
in a round capsule. Found in mid- to south
Lakeland in damp grassland, and in marshy
places throughout the N Pennines.
   The pimpernels were once used against
melancholy, epilepsy, fevers and kidney
conditions.

RAGGED ROBIN

ROUGH ROBIN (CUMBERLAND),
THUNDER FLOWER, BACHELORS' BUTTONS

Height 30–76cm/12–30in ❀ **May–August**

Lychnis flos-cuculi
Gk *lychnis*, lamp, or campion; L *flos-cuculi*,
cuckoo flower

An upright perennial of wet meadows, fens
and woods. Has short hairy non-flowering
stems and taller flowering stems. Stalked hairy
leaves are spoon-shaped at base, and opposite,
narrow, lance-shaped above. Distinctive pink
(or white) flowers have 5 deeply cut petals
each divided into 4 narrow lobes, giving a
ragged appearance. Copita-shaped capsule
bears brown seeds. Found in wet meadows to
great heights.

Gerard writes: 'Not used in medicine or
nourishment, but they serve for garlands and
crowns, and to deck up gardens.' Old belief
that picking flowers incurred a thunderstorm,
bunches hung in byres brought lightning.

REDSHANK

REDLEG, PERSICARIA

Height 15–45cm/6–18in ❀ **June–October**

Polygonum maculosa
L *poly*, many; *gony*, knee; *maculosa*, spotted

A straggly waterside annual of acid soils.
Erect, sometimes sprawling, hairless reddish
stems have alternate, thin lance-shaped leaves
with a dark blotch on the upper sides, silky
underneath, rising from brown cup-like
sheaths. Pink 5-petalled flowers crowd up
short spikes rising from the upper sheaths.
Fruits are black glossy nutlets. A common
wasteland weed found at all altitudes in the
region.

Medieval belief that this was the herb
under the crucifixion tree, the dark spots
on the leaves showing where Christ's blood
spilled. Shetlanders used it for a yellow dye.

VALERIAN, MARSH

Height 10–30cm/4–12in ❀ May–June

Valeriana dioica
L *Valeriana* from Valeria, a Roman province
in western Hungary, or after Valerius, who
used it as a medicine, or *valere*, to be healthy;
dioica, male and female on separate plants

A short perennial of wet places with a
creeping root system from which rise erect
flowering stems, reddish at base. They bear
2 opposite pairs of long-stalked spoon-shaped
leaves below, and 2 opposite pairs of deeply
divided pinnate leaves above. The flowers are
in terminal stalked clusters, the male larger
and deeper pink, the female smaller, looser
and paler, on separate plants. Found in wet
places on limy or neutral soils, being most
common in S and E Lakeland and all over
the Pennines.

Sometimes used to augment apothecaries'
Common Valerian, but individually inferior
so seldom, if ever, used as a herbal medicine.

WILLOWHERB, MARSH

Height 15–38cm/6–15in ❀ June–August

Epilobium palustre
Gk *epi*, upon; *lobos*, pod; L *palustre*, of marshes

A hairy or smooth perennial of wet acid,
usually upland places. A slender round stem
rises from an underground stolon, and it bears
mostly opposite narrow lance-shaped little-
toothed unstalked leaves with basal bracts.
Pale pink or white Willowherb flowers held
in a loose head. Plumed seeds are wind and
water dispersed. Common in marshy uplands,
wet flushes, lake and beck margins throughout
the region. Only slightly less frequent in
Yorkshire Dales at lower levels.

WILLOWHERB, NEW ZEALAND

Height 5–10cm/2–4in ❁ June–July

Epilobium brunnescens
Gk *epi*, on; *lobos*, pod; L *brunescens*, browning

A ground-hugging perennial with slim, creeping stems that root as they creep. Leaves opposite, stalked and toothed, oval to round, hairless, turning a coppery-green as they age. Single, nodding, long-stalked flowers are held erect, each with 4 notched pale pink petals with reddish sepals surmounting the typical willowherb fruit pod. Parachute seeds are wind dispersed.

Accidentally imported in New Zealand wool bales which, when opened, released seed parachutes that were borne by wind to damp acid upland areas and germinated. This theory is borne out by its prevalence around airfields in the south east used during World War II by incoming New Zealand troops, who carried the seeds in their boots.

BROOKLIME

LIMEWORT, WATER PURPLE (CUMBERLAND)

Height 20–60cm/8–24in ❀ May–September

Veronica beccabunga
After St Veronica who accompanied Christ
to the cross; ON *bekkr*, beck; *bung*, block
Brooklime from OE *brok*, brook, and L *limus*,
lime (plaster)

A sprawling fleshy perennial of wet places.
Hollow creeping often rooting stems give rise
to erect sometimes reddish flowering stems
with opposite short-stalked, bluntly toothed,
fleshy leaves. Bright blue white-eyed flowers,
with 4 unequal petals, rise from leaf joints in
opposite slim-stalked spikes of up to 30. Fruits
in rounded capsules. Very common in ponds,
becks and ditches in all but the highest
Lakeland Fells.

   Leaves edible, not very palatable in salads
but once used for scurvy. Used in some diet
drinks, and as a blood purge. In medieval
times used for gout and other swellings.

BUTTERWORT

MARSH VIOLET, BOG VIOLET

Height 5–10cm/2–4in ❀ May–July

Pinguicula vulgaris
L *pinguis*, fat (greasy leaves); *vulgaris*, common

A ground-hugging perennial of wet places.
The basal rosette is composed of broad-
oblong, sticky yellowish-green leaves with
inrolled edges. The leaves entrap small
insects, which are digested to supply minerals
to feed the plant. Single violet-coloured
flowers top an erect unbranched stem. 3 lower
petals extended backwards in a pointed spur
form a lip with a white patch, and 2 upper
petals a hood. Fruits in a round pod.

   Little used now medicinally, but once
popular for coughs, chapped hands and as a
purgative. Homeopathic remedy for whooping
cough, throat irritations, colds and coughs. As
an ointment, it was used to cure sores on cows'
udders. In NE England, leaves were added to
milk to curdle or thicken it.

FORGET-ME-NOT, WATER

SCORPION GRASS

Height 7.5–30cm/3–12in ❀ June–October

Myosotis scorpioides
Gk *mus*, mouse; *otos*, ear; L *scorpioides*, like a scorpion's tail

A creeping perennial rising from a submerged rootstock. Angular stems with close-pressed hairs bear unstalked alternate roughly oblong leaves. Short-stalked 5-petalled notched flowers with white guide-lines and a yellow eye are borne on slender stems, coiled like a scorpion to uncoil as buds burst into bloom. Black nutlets in sepal cups spread loosely up the flowering stems.

Gerard maintained that its flowerhead was a signature of its ability to counter the stings of venomous beasts such as scorpions, snakes, mad dogs, etc. The plant has been used in an ointment for cuts and wounds, spots and boils.

LUNGWORT

JACOB'S COAT, JERUSALEM COWSLIP, SOLDIERS AND SAILORS, MARY-SPILT-THE-MILK

Height up to 30cm/12in ❀ March–June

Pulmonaria officinalis
L *pulmo*, lung; *officinalis*, used medicinally

A rough hairy perennial with long-stalked basal leaves, pointed and egg-shaped, and unstalked upper leaves clasping stem. Terminal clusters of blue-purple 5-petalled flowers, pink in bud. Egg-shaped nutlets develop in corolla. Probably a garden escape in the UK.

The doctrine of signatures suggested lung-like leaves would cure lung diseases. Infusions used for coughs and lung catarrh, bronchitis and diarrhoea. Young leaves can be used in salads, soups or stews. (Note that the Lungwort sold by pharmacies is not this species, but a moss known as Lung Moss or Oak Lungs.)

MILKWORT, HEATH

THYME-LEAVED MILKWORT,
ROGATION FLOWER, CROSS FLOWER

Height 5–10cm/2–4in   ❀ May–September

Polygala serpyllifolia
Gk *poly*, much; *gala*, milk; L *serpyllifolia*,
thyme-leaved

A slender hairless perennial like Common
Milkwort but preferring heaths or dry
acid grassland. The stems rise erectly from
the roots bearing opposite pairs of oval to
elliptical, hairless leaves near the base, and
similar alternate leaves above. Flowers 3–10,
carried in loose terminal spikes, blue, pink or
white with 5 sepals, 3 minute green and 2
large blue, fused into a frilled trumpet that
almost hides the petals. Small seed capsules
enclosed by the persisting sepal wings.

Infusions of the plant were supposed to
increase mothers' milk. Flowering around
Rogationtide it was traditionally carried in
maidens' nosegays and garlands.

SCABIOUS, DEVIL'S BIT

Height 15–100cm/6–40in   ❀ July–October

Sucissa pratensis
L *sucissa*, abruptly broken off; *pratensis*,
of meadows

A perennial herb with a short upright root,
abruptly ended as if bitten off. A rosette of
stalked elliptical leaves, sometimes purplish,
supports slender, hairy, upright stems with
narrower, opposite leaves, sometimes toothed.
At the top it carries one largish hemispherical
head of tightly packed lilac to dark blue
funnel-shaped florets, with smaller flowers
rising below on slender stalks from leaf bract
joints on either side of the stem. A wet
grassland plant at all altitudes.

Still used in infusions for coughs, fevers,
internal inflammation, to cleanse blood,
and as a warm decoction to remove scurf and
dandruff. Culpeper prescribed boiled root for
snakebite, swollen throats, wounds, plague,
shortness of breath and lung diseases.

SHEEPSBIT

Height 5–50cm/2–20in   ❀ May–August

Jasione montana
Gk *Jasione*, plant's name, healer; L *montana*,
of mountains

A hairy biennial with many hairy erect stems
bearing small narrow wavy short-stalked
leaves spirally (not opposite as in Scabiouses).
The upper half of the stems are leafless
bearing a single terminal, globular, unrayed
blue sometimes white flower with a ruff of
green bracts. It prefers drier acid ground to
Devil's Bit Scabious, and is common on sand
dunes, roadsides and hedgerows west of the
Pennines.

   The bruised leaves exude an unpleasant
odour and picking these flowers is said to give
one warts. Gerard said it was good for coughs,
shortness of breath, and pains in the sides and
chest. Also a remedy for snakebite.

Clubmosses are not flowers but primitive, specially adapted plants that reproduce by spores and bulbils or vegetatively rather than by seeds

CLUBMOSS, ALPINE

Height 5–10cm/2–4in ✸ June–August

Lycopodium alpinum
Gk *lykos*, wolf; L *podium*, foot; *alpinum*, of the mountains

A prostrate creeping perennial with tufts of upright branches rising from square, branched stems. These are tightly covered by fleshy, pointed greyish scale-like leaves giving the appearance of a snake. Some of the upright branches terminate in greyish-green scaled 'cones' that produce the spores. This plant is to be found fairly frequently in the western and northern Lakeland Fells but rarely in the Pennines. It is also found at high levels in Snowdonia and Scottish and Irish mountains. It grows on short, grazed grassland.

CLUBMOSS, FIR

UPRIGHT FIR CLUBMOSS

Height 5–10cm/2–4in ✸ June–August

Urostachys selago
L *uro*, tailed; Gk *stachys*, spike; *selago*, of the Lycopodium family

An evergreen tufted perennial with almost erect frequently forked stems rooting at the base and rising from a creeping stem. Untoothed narrow pointed leaves crowd up the stem, but not as tightly as Alpine Clubmoss, and form bulbils near the top. Spore capsules are located sporadically near the bases of leaves. Reproduction almost exclusively vegetatively by the bulbils. Fairly common on grassy, rocky, acid hillsides in the Lakes and Pennines, where it is often found uprooted by sheep or boots. Seen in screes on Cross Fell.

Fresh leaves are used by homeopathists as an effective laxative. They also kill worms.

CLUBMOSS, LESSER

Height 2–3cm/1–2in ❀ June–September

Selaginella selaginoides
L *selaginella*, Pliny's name for lycopodium;
selaginoides, like selaginella

A low perennial with branched stems rising
weakly from creeping stems. All stems are
thickly clad with small toothed lance-shaped
spirally arranged leaves, and terminate
with green spore cones. It is often hidden
by surrounding grasses, and can easily be
mistaken for a moss. A fairly common
mountain plant of flushes, rocky slopes and
ledges in the Lakes and Pennines. Particularly
noticeable on tracksides in Widdybank Fell
on the approach to Cauldron Snout.
  No known pharmaceutical uses.

CLUBMOSS, STAG'S HORN

Height 5–10cm/2–4in ❀ June–September

Lycopodium clavatum
Gk *lyco*, wolf; L *podium*, foot; *clavatum*,
club-shaped

A creeping perennial, stems often up to
several metres long, rooting frequently at
joints. Closely set green toothed leaves
tapering to white points hide the stems, some
of which extend narrowly upwards, usually
twin-forked, to bear terminal cones covered
with scattered, yellow, toothed scales.
Commoner in the Pennines than the Lake
District where it is found in the west and
central Fells.
  Used since medieval times as a diuretic, to
flush out kidney stones and against gastritis
and indigestion. The water-resistant spores
were used to coat pills, and to relieve irritated
or itchy skin. The spores ignite explosively
and have been used in fireworks.

DOCK, CLUSTERED

SHARP DOCK

Height 30–60cm/12–24in ✽ June–October

Rumex conglomeratus
L *rumex*, sorrel family; *conglomeratus*, clustered

A stiff perennial rising from a long white
taproot. Slightly zig-zag, erect, reddish stems
bear long broad pointed leaves, rounded at
the base, and sometimes waisted. Insignificant
green flowers are carried in whorls on much-
branched, long-stalked, leafy clusters. Fruits
have 3 longish warts that turn red when ripe.
It is considered a farmyard and garden weed,
and is common in lowland areas on damp
ground.
   Has been used as a laxative, for blood and
skin diseases and diphtheria, but now seldom
used.

DOCK, CURLED

YELLOW DOCK

Height 50–100cm/20–40in ✽ June–October

Rumex crispus
L *rumex*, sorrel; *crispus*, wrinkly, wavy

A perennial plant with a tough, persistent,
carrot-like root. An upright branched stem
bears alternate short-stalked lance-shaped
leaves with very wavy edges. Leafy loose
spikes bear dense clusters of tiny green flowers
in whorls. 3-sided fruits enclosed by 3 green
wings. It is scheduled as an injurious
agricultural weed, and grows in any soils at
any altitude up to about 350m/1,150ft.
   The leaves were once eaten as a spring
tonic. Only the root is now considered to
be of any use, mainly as a gentle laxative,
a detoxificant, and to assist with liver and
skin diseases.

Mosses, like ferns, reproduce by spores. They form an important element in the natural progression of plant-life. Algae and lichens are the earliest recognisable plant forms that inhabit the ground, and start the process of breaking down underlying surfaces to enable the slightly more advanced mosses to gain a foothold. They have no roots, only stems that form root-like rhizoids. When ripe, spores are forcibly ejected to form new plants on the surrounding surface. Male cells migrate over wet surfaces to fertilise separate female receptacles and create new plants. When mosses die, their waterlogged remains cannot decay, but build up to form layers of peat.

The commonest form of peat is created by Sphagnum Moss spp, whose capacity to retain moisture makes it an ideal growing medium for nurserymen and gardeners. Its cheap and easy exploitation has decimated blanket bogs that took millennia to develop.

MOSS, FEATHER

TAMARISK MOSS

Height 2–10cm/1–4in

Thuidium tamariscinum
Gk *thuidium*, plant name, like Thuja; Hebrew *tamaris*, sweeping broom, or like the feathery, pale green foliage of Tamarisk

An attractive delicate moss that colonises fallen trees, rotting wood and damp rocks on shady, woodland floors. The bright green or gold stems bear triangular, feather-like leaves that form a thick thatch to aid decomposition of the host before it can support more advanced forms of plant life. Fruit capsules are very rarely produced in springtime, reproduction is mainly from creeping stems.

MOSS, SPHAGNUM SPP

BOG MOSS

Stems up to 25cm/10in

Sphagnum cymbifolium
Gk *sphagnos*, a moss; L *cymbi*, boat-like;
folium, leaved

There are many species of Sphagnum moss,
ranging in colour from pale green, almost
white to dull reds. They are made up of
individual weak stems with spongy, spirally
arranged leaves permeated with many
capillary tubes that soak up rain. Some species
form crowded clusters at the top of the stems.
Fruiting capsules may appear in early summer.
Sphagnum mosses grow on acid soils, have
low mineral food requirements, and can live
on rainwater alone.

Because of its great power of absorption,
Sphagnum moss has long been used for
dressing battle wounds, e.g. at Clontarf (1014)
and Flodden Field (1513). It was used with
garlic for field dressings in both World Wars.

MOSS, STAR

HAIR MOSS

Height 2–40cm/1–16in ❀ **Spores ripen in summer**

Polytrichum commune
Gk *polytrichum*, many-haired; L *commune*,
common

Erect dark green toothed fine lance-shaped
leaves are borne on long wiry stems to form
large loose cushions in wet heaths, bogs,
moorland and woodland streams. Its long-
stalked, 4-sided spore capsules produced in
summer, have hairy, yellowish caps when
young. Male plants bear a pinkish tuft at
their tips. Common, with many variants
in wet heathland, bogs and moorland.

Little used medicinally, but stuffed into
beds and pillows in Lapland.

MYRTLE, BOG

GALE, SWEET GALE (NORTHERN ENGLAND),
GOLD WITHY, FLEAWOOD (NORTHUMBERLAND)

Height 60–120cm/24–48in   April–May

Myrica gale
Gk *myrika*, tamarix or fragrance; *gale* from
gagel, OE plant name

An aromatic deciduous shrub with erect
reddish stems that bear greenish cone-like
male catkins and smaller red female catkins
on separate plants before leaves develop.
Unstalked long thin toothed glossy-green
leaves are downy with yellow glands below
that exude aromatic resins. The fruit is a dry,
flattened nut.

Infusions used against worms, gastric and
skin conditions. In N England and Scotland it
was used for flea-proof bedding and to protect
linen from moths. Crofters hung it indoors to
deter midges. Sprigs were carried by brides,
including Queen Victoria and Princess Anne,
and first communicants to invoke happiness.

NETTLE, STINGING

HOKEY POKEY, DEVIL'S PLAYTHING

Height 25–150cm/10–60in   May–September

Urtica dioica
L *uro*, to burn; *dioica*, in two houses (male
and female on separate plants)
Nettle from OE *netele*

Stout, creeping, rooting, yellow stolons project
hairy, upright, square, reddish-brown stems.
Opposite pairs of pointed heart-shaped, toothed
leaves covered with stinging hairs. Crowded,
greenish male flowers droop in long catkin-like
spikes, while the female flowers hang in clusters.
Pollen is released by the male flowers in
explosive bursts. Seeds are hairy and bulb-like.

Plants contain silicic, formic and acetic
acids, iron, glucoquinine, histamine and
chlorophyll. Diuretic, anti-rheumatic, a tonic
and blood stimulant, used for anaemia, jaundice
and nervous and physical exhaustion. Used
for making cloth from the Bronze Age to the
nineteenth century, until ousted by flax.

PLANTAIN, HOARY

LAMB'S EAR (CUMBERLAND)

Height 7.5–30cm/3–12in ❀ May–August

Plantago media
L *planta*, sole of foot; *media*, middle-sized

A greyish perennial of lime-rich soils. The
leaves form a basal rosette and are broad oval,
narrowing to a winged stalk with prominent
ribs and covered with white hairs. Erect hairy
stalks bear a dense cylindrical spike of grey-
green flowers with prominent pale purple
stamens. The only plantain with a delicate
perfume that attracts insects. Its seeds are
very popular with small birds. Common on
limestone up to 450m/1,500ft.
   Gerard writes: 'The juice dropped in the
eyes cools the heat and inflammation thereof.
The seeds boiled in milk are laxative and
demulcent. The leaves rubbed into the
stems of fruit trees afflicted with blight
effect a ready cure.'

PLANTAIN, RATSTAIL

GREATER PLANTAIN, BIRD'S MEAT,
CANARY FLOWER, COMMON PLANTAIN

Height 7.5–45cm/3–18in ❀ June–September

Plantago major
L *plantaginem*, sole of foot (hugs the ground);
major, greater

A depressed often hairy perennial with a
basal rosette of stalked wavy oval leaves with
prominent veins underneath. Tiny yellow-green
flowers with conspicuous purple anthers, are
borne in single slender spikes, the flowerheads
as tall as the stems. The fruits are 4–16 seeds
in a 2-celled capsule. Common virtually
everywhere.
   Sympathetic magic suggested its toughness
would heal crushing, tearing and bruising.
Dioscorides wrote that it was good for wounds,
sores, ulcers and scrofula. Also used for urinary
and bowel complaints, but not as effective as
Ribwort Plantain. Seed heads sold as feed for
cage birds.

PLANTAIN, RIBWORT

SOLDIERS (CUMBERLAND), RIBGRASS
(NORTHERN ENGLAND), FIGHTIE COCKS
(NORTH-EAST ENGLAND), HARDHEADS

Height 7.5–45cm/3–18in ❀ April–August

Plantago lanceolata
L *plantago*, sole of the foot; *lanceolata*, lance-shaped

A perennial with an ascending basal rosette of many narrow, hairy leaves slightly toothed and ridged with 3–5 prominent ribs. Several flower-heads rise erectly on ridged hairy stalks much longer than the dense, 1–5cm/½–2in cylindrical spikes of browny-green flowers with white or yellow stamens. Fruits are tiny 2-sided capsules. Ubiquitous.

Pollen research reveals it spread rapidly in Great Britain after Neolithic deforestation. Once considered a most valuable herb for healing various conditions and still used in some bronchitis and cough medicines, and liver and intestinal tonics.

PLANTAIN, SEA

SHEEPS' HERB (WALES)

Height up to 12.5cm/5in ❀ June–August

Plantago maritima
L *planta*, sole of foot; *maritima*, coastal

A spreading perennial with several closely packed, writhing rosettes of thick, fleshy narrow grass-like leaves with one or two teeth. Browny-green flowers are held in 2–7.5cm/1–3in cylindrical spikes on smooth erect stems. A fairly common plant of coastal areas and not uncommon on the limestone hills and rich flushes in the mountains of the northern and central Pennines.

It has been cultivated in North Wales as sheep fodder, hence its local name. Another Welsh name for it translates as 'suet producer'.

RUSH, SOFT

Height 30–150cm/12–60in ❀ June–August

Juncus effusus
L *juncus*, rush or binder (basketry); *effusus*,
spread out (flowers)

A grass-like plant of wet places. Glossy green
cylindrical leaves and flower stems with
brown sheaths at the base rise erectly from
dense perennial tufts. The finely ridged stems
have a spongy cellular pith that can be
extracted when mature. Heads of tiny green
flowers on short stalks are borne in a loose
brownish cluster at one side of the stem
a little from the top. Common up to
850m/2,800ft on badly drained land.

Mixed with wine, a concoction made from
soaking the leaves in water was used as a
cough cure. Long valued for use as rushlights.
After soaking in water, the rush was carefully
peeled, the pith extracted in long strips then
dipped in wax or grease to provide a good,
clear, almost smokeless light.

SORREL, MOUNTAIN

Height 10–25cm/4–10in ❀ June–August

Oxyria digyna
Gk *oxys*, sharp, acidic; *digyna*, with 2 styles or
carpels

A tufted hairless perennial of rock ledges and
damp grassy upland places. Long-stalked
fleshy kidney-shaped leaves with wavy edges
spring straight from the roots. One or two are
on the erect hairless stems below the sorrel-
like spikes of tiny red-edged green flowers that
develop into 2-valved fruits. The red edges
contain anthocyanin, common to all plants
but usually hidden by green chlorophyll. In
upland plants growing with high ultra-violet
radiation the red acts as a screen to the
harmful rays. Found only in the higher
Lakeland Fells, Snowdonia and Scotland.

Culpeper says: 'The leaves are as sour as
the common, and may be used with it both
in medicines and salad.'

SORREL, SHEEP'S

FIELD SORREL

Height 7.5–25cm/3–10in   ❀ May–August

Rumex acetosella
L *rumere*, to suck (leaves for refreshment);
acetosella, acidic

A low tufted perennial with a creeping rootstock giving rise to many branched, erect, flower stems. Stalked leaves have a paper-like sheath at the base and are shaped like arrows with the basal lobe outspread and pointing upwards. The upper unleaved branched flower stems bear small flowers; yellow-anthered male, and whitish-green female on separate plants. Fruits held in a 3-sided reddish capsule.

A salad vegetable, detoxifying, diuretic and gently laxative. Juice from leaves once used for urinary and kidney complaints. Excessive use may prove poisonous, and can cause milk fever in cows. Recently advocated as a major ingredient in a herbal cancer remedy.

ADDER'S TONGUE

CHRIST'S SPEAR

Height 5–23cm/2–8in ❀ May–September

Ophioglossum vulgatum
Gk *ophios*, snake; *glossa*, tongue; L *vulgatum*,
common

A primitive fern that grows in sandy coastal
areas, in limestone pastures and upland
mining areas. Solitary round stems consist of
a fleshy, veined, sterile, green blade sheathing
(like Cuckoo Pint) a taller fleshy erect fertile
spike, the upper part of which has 16– 40
sunken sporangia (spore capsules) on either
side.

Once much used to heal wounds in a
preparation called Green Oil of Charity. The
juice of its leaves was used for internal wounds
and bleeding. As indicated by its name and
because it looks like a snake's tongue, it was
believed to be an antidote to snakebite.

BRACKEN

BRAKES

Height 20–200cm/8–80in ❀ May–October

Pteridium aquilinum
Gk *pteris*, fern (from *pteron*, a feather);
L *aquilinum*, eagle (stem cut obliquely at base
resembles an eagle, according to Linnaeus)

A deciduous perennial patch-forming fern
rising from a long stout hairy creeping
rhizome. The only branched fern, its sturdy
erect stems rise singly from the rootstock and
bear branching fronds, roughly triangular,
with stalks half as long as the fronds. Spore
cases borne in thin lines along the back edges
of the leaflets, spores ripening July to August.

Uses included worm-killer and gastric
cleanser. Smoke from smouldering fronds for
sciatica and to repel midges. Plant also burned
for potash. Spores considered carcinogenic.
Toxins in mature fronds make it unpalatable
to grazing animals. New shoots, blanched,
peeled and boiled, can be eaten.

FERN, HARD

LADDER FERN

Height 10–38cm/4–15in ❀ June–August

Blechnum spicant
From Gk *blechnon*, a fern; L *spicant*, tufted

A short, tufted wintergreen fern with a small
scaly rootstock with spreading rootlets. Sterile
wintergreen shiny leaves like ladders spread
along the ground. Later, taller brownish fertile
fronds rise erectly form the base like slim fish-
bones, their stalks half the frond length, with
spore cases in lines either side of the leaflet
midriffs. They die back in winter after the
spores have been shed. A plant of damp acid
woodland, hedges and peaty pastures, and
mountain beck sides. Sometimes grows under
Ling or in Bracken.
  No known culinary or medicinal uses.

FERN, PARSLEY

Height low to 75cm/29in ❀ June–August

Cryptogramma crispa
Gk *krypto*, to hide; *gramma*, line (of spore
cases); L *crispa*, crisped

A short deciduous mountain fern rising from
a scaly tuft covered with dead leaf bases. A
dense spirally arranged outer tuft of much-
divided sterile fronds 5–15cm/2–6in long
and resembling Parsley, cradles narrower
and longer fertile fronds. These are up to
25cm/10in long with narrow club-shaped
leaflets, their edges curled back almost hiding
the spore cases round the underside margins.
An upland plant of acid screes, rocks and
walls, common in Wales, N England and
Scotland, but probably at its most prevalent
in Cumbria.

POLYPODY

Height 5–30cm/2–12in ❀ **July–August**

Polypodium vulgare
Gk *poly*, many; *podos*, foot; L *vulgare*, common

A low creeping wintergreen fern of damp
woodlands and dry stone walls, and often as
an epiphyte on oak trees. It has a creeping
woody scaly rhizome with hair-like roots
beneath. Flat shiny dark green broad fish-
bone fronds rise alternately from the upper
side of the stock on stalks about a third or
a half the length of the blade. Large round
spore cases are in rows either side of the
midriffs. New fronds are produced in early
summer.

Dioscorides used it to purge phlegm, and in
a plaster for sore fingers. In medieval times it
was used to cure whooping cough, rheumatic
conditions, jaundice, dropsy and scurvy.
Culpeper recommended it as a gentle purge.
Burnt leaves are rich in potash.

Morning mist on the Lakeland fells

WALKS

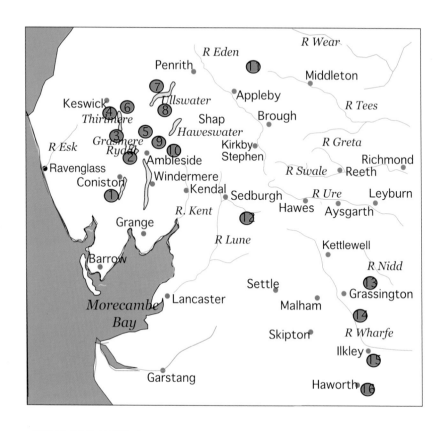

SYMBOLS USED IN THE MAPS

～～～	Road	▲	Hilltop
- - - - -	Track or bridleway	▲	Youth Hostel
━━━	River or beck	⬡	Viewpoint
- - - -	Walking route	■	Building
～～	Wall or hedge	♁	Church or chapel
┼┼┼┼┼┼	Railway	Ⓟ	Parking
▼▼▼▼	Upper / Lower Slopes	ⓌⒸ	Toilets

WALKS

		km	miles	hours
1	BEACON TARN & FELL	8.5	5 1/4	3–3 1/2
2	LOUGHRIGG FELL & TARN	8	4 1/2	2 1/2–3
3	EASEDALE TARN & SILVER HOW	10	6 1/4	4–5
4	WATENDLATH & DOCK TARN	7.5	4 3/4	3–3 1/2
5A	TONGUE GILL & GRISEDALE TARN	6.5	4	3–4
5B	TONGUE GILL & GRISEDALE TARN	8	5	3–4
6	HIGH RIGG & ST JOHN'S VALE	12	7 1/2	4–5
7	GOWBARROW FELL & AIRA FORCE	8	5	2 1/2–3
8	HAYESWATER & ANGLE TARN	11	7	4–4 1/2
9	TROUTBECK TONGUE	12	7 1/2	4 1/2–5 1/2
10	WHINFELL BEACON & BORROWDALE	14.5	9	4 1/2–5
11	KIRKLAND & CROSS FELL	14.5	9	4 1/2–5 1/2
12	WHERNSIDE	14.5	9	4 1/2–5 1/2
13	GRIMWITH RESERVOIR	7	4 1/2	2 1/2–3
14	BARDEN FELL & STRID WOOD	14.5	9	4 1/2–5 1/2
15	ILKLEY MOOR	11	7	4–4 1/2
16	WUTHERING HEIGHTS & HAWORTH MOOR	12	7 1/2	4–5

INTRODUCTION

The walks have been specially chosen to ensure the discovery of different species where they are to be seen, often in local abundance, however rare they may be nationally. All the flowers in this book are accompanied with simple non-technical descriptions, including size and preferred habitats; the flowering charts, specific to Northern England, should further assist in identification. As in Volume 1, *Limestone Flowers*, all the species are to be seen within two metres of public or permitted footpaths, thus eliminating any need to trespass to find them. On common land, such as Torver Common and Barden Fell, access is unrestricted, subject to avoiding any disturbance to nesting birds or trampling on rare plants.

In addition, the routes selected offer picturesque landscapes, often from an elevated viewpoint, making them classic walks in their own right.

The maps have been drawn to show only relevant landmarks and features, even down to field walls (thin black lines) in cases where finding the route might be difficult. Walking routes are indicated by dotted red lines, with red arrows to indicate preferred directions, but since all walks are circular they can be taken in the opposite direction, depending on weather conditions. Exposed upland paths, for example, should be done with a following wind, while strong headwinds need to be countered by sheltered valley or woodland paths.

The majority of the walks would be classified as easy. Times given are based on an average rate of two miles per hour, enough to allow for refreshment breaks and stops for detailed inspection of plants. Most of the maps have sufficient detail to enable the routes to be shortened or extended if desired.

The best footwear is boots or strong shoes with grooved soles, although for lower-level walks trainers or Wellingtons would suffice. Sudden changes of weather are possible at all times, so waterproof and windproof garments are recommended. Food is a personal consideration, but on a hot day water or soft drinks are essential, since beck water is often polluted by animals and should not be drunk.

In 1997 the Ordnance Survey issued a new series (NS) of Outdoor Leisure Maps that considerably extended the boundaries of the old series (OS). References are given to both.

Opposite: The Strid on the River Wharfe, Walk 14

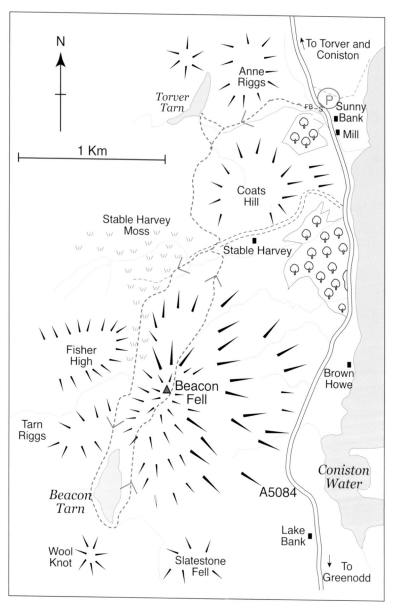

Map: use OS Outdoor Leisure 7, English Lakes, SW

WALK 1 ◆ BEACON TARN & FELL

Distance 8.5 km / 5¹/₄ miles
Time 3–3¹/₂ hours

Park at SD 288926, on the wide verge
of the A5084 just N of Sunny Bank
Mill. Cross road then follow footpath
over stile opposite then footbridge up
to fork near top; go R to Torver Tarn.
Then take a well-used footpath S to
Stable Harvey Lane. Go R for 200m
then take footpath that rises through
boggy hollows to the W of Beacon Fell
then descends to Beacon Tarn. Carry
on to S end of tarn, cross Tarn Beck
and follow footpath up the S ridge
of Beacon Fell to the summit, 250m/
836ft, which yields panoramic views.
Continue NE to a fork, go L to drop
down to Stable Harvey Lane, and
follow outward route back to start.

LOOK OUT FOR

April	Gorse, Bog Myrtle, Bilberry
May	Cranberry, Bogbean, Heath Milkwort
June	Butterwort, Bog Pimpernel, Bell Heather
July	Water Lobelia, Sundew, Northern Marsh Orchid
August	Ling, Oblong-leaved Sundew, Sneezewort
September	Gorse, Angelica, Devil's Bit Scabious
October	Tormentil, Lesser Spearwort, Autumnal Hawkbit

Birds to be seen include Yellow
Hammer, Meadow Pipit,
Stonechat, Swallow, House
Martin, Wheatear, Raven and
Willow Warbler. Lizards can be
spotted by the observant.

Torver is from ON *torf*, turf or peat, and ON *erg*, pasture

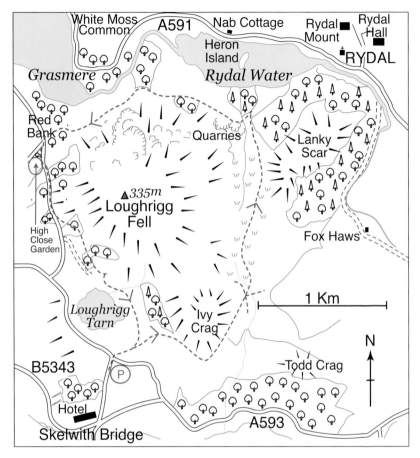

Map: use OS Outdoor Leisure 7, English Lakes SE

WALK 2 ◆ LOUGHRIGG FELL & TARN

Distance 7 km / 4¹/₂ miles
Time 2¹/₂–3 hours

From Ambleside on the A593 take R fork past Ellers to road off to L, on the corner of which is a recessed parking place (SD 346040). Cross Red Bank road bearing R then soon L along a farm access road past cottages to gates. Go straight ahead, signed Ambleside. The path skirts Ivy Crag where a short detour L gives splendid views. Continue on to boggy area and go straight ahead N, eventually descending to a quarry track near Rydal Water. Go L up to quarries, which are worthy of exploration, then continue on along Loughrigg Terrace to Red Bank road. Follow road to L, forking L where a road goes off to Dungeon Ghyll. Continue down to a stile with footpath sign on L, pass behind house and through small wood to a lane overlooking Loughrigg Tarn, which follow back to start.

LOOK OUT FOR

April	Golden Saxifrage, Coltsfoot, Daffodil
May	Butterwort, Bilberry, Yellow Mountain Saxifrage
June	Sundew, Tormentil, New Zealand Willowherb
July	Bog Asphodel, Bell Heather, Cotton Grass
August	Cross-leaved Heath, Heath Milkwort, Sneezewort
September	Grass of Parnassus, Marsh Willowherb, Tormentil
October	Lesser Spearwort, Devil's Bit Scabious, Smooth Hawksbeard

Birds to be seen or heard include Meadow Pipit, Chaffinch, Wren, Buzzard, Magpie, Jackdaw, Green Woodpecker, Mallard, Coot, Mute Swan.

Loughrigg from OScan *lauk-hoursyggr*, ridge where leeks grow
Rydal, dale where rye grows
Ambleside, from ON *amelr*, river sandbank, and ON *saetr*, summer shieling or hill pasture

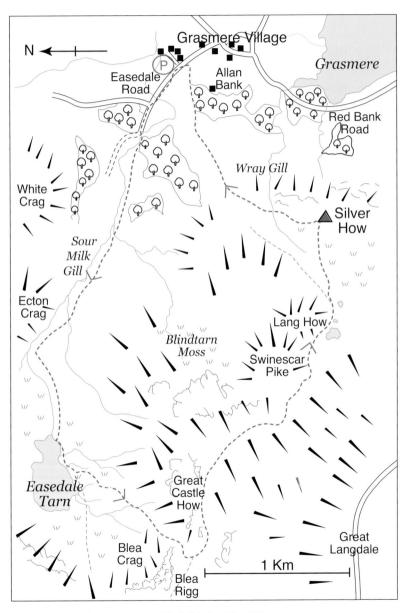

Map: use OS Outdoor Leisure 7 or 6 English Lakes SE or SW

WALK 3
EASEDALE TARN & SILVER HOW

Distance 10 km / 6¼ miles
Time 4–5 hours

Park in Easedale Road car park,
Grasmere (NY 335079). Cross road to
stile, go R along footpath then road to
bridleway on L signed Easedale Tarn. A
well-used path continues directly ahead
past Sour Milk Gill and waterfalls to
Easedale Tarn. About half way along
the S side of the tarn at a small cairn an
indistinct path to the L skirts the L side
of a small hummock and continues up
fairly steeply to a crossing path at the
crest. Follow this footpath L, passing
Great Castle How on L, and meander
roughly E to SE past Swinescar Pike
and tarns below Lang How, then
straight on to Silver How summit from
which there is a spectacular panorama.
Leave the summit bearing W and pick
up footpath to cross Wray Gill and
descend to road, then R, taking new
footpath on L just before Allen Bank,
back to start.

LOOK OUT FOR

April	Golden Saxifrage, Fir Clubmoss, Dog Violet
May	Tormentil, Sheep's Sorrel, Butterwort
June	Bogbean, Lousewort, Heath Milkwort
July	Climbing Corydalis, Bog Asphodel, Lesser Spearwort
August	Bell Heather, Ling, Cross-leaved Heath
September	Devil's Bit Scabious, Water Pepper, Parsley Fern

How from OScand *haughours*, hill
Grasmere from OScand *gres*, grass, and OE *mere*, lake
William Wordsworth, his wife Mary and sister Dorothy lived for 14 years in Grasmere at
Dove Cottage, Allan Bank and the Rectory, before moving a few miles to Rydal Mount where
William died 37 years later at the age of 80. They knew intimately and loved the area, which
inspired many of William's writings. They were all particularly attached to Easedale, which
they referred to as The Dark Quarter because from Dove Cottage it seemed continually
swathed in mist, cloud or rain. Yet it was beside the Gill that Wordsworth wrote many of
his verses, possibly because Easedale afforded a tranquil and undisturbed retreat in which
he could exercise his creative ideas.

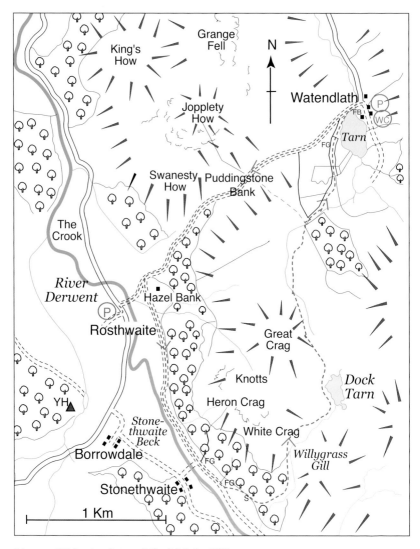

Map: use OS Outdoor Leisure 4, English Lakes NW

WALK 4 ◆ WATENDLATH & DOCK TARN

Distance 7.5 km / 4³/₄ miles
Time 3–3¹/₂ hours

Park in Rosthwaite National Trust car park off the lane opposite the post office (NY 258147). Cross road and take track to L signed Hazel Bank. Turn R before this hotel and follow bridleway signed Stonethwaite. After passing Stonethwaite track on R, continue along bridleway now signed Greenup Edge. Through the second gateway, take footpath on L rising into woodland then climbing steeply in zig-zags. At the wood top follow a cairned path beside Willygrass Gill to Dock Tarn. The path continues along the west of the tarn and descends to a sign offering Rosthwaite via Puddingstone Bank or Watendlath (toilets and refreshments) to R. Leave Watendlath over bridge and up track L back to Rosthwaite.

LOOK OUT FOR

April	Golden Saxifrage, Bog Myrtle, Bilberry
May	Spring Sedge, Heath Milkwort, Cotton Grass
June	Heath Spotted Orchid, Butterwort, Lousewort
July	Sundew, Tormentil, Yellow Pimpernel
August	Ling, Water Pepper, Lousewort
September	Spearwort, Sneezewort, Grass of Parnassus

Dock Tarn hosts Dragonflies and Damselflies. Birds include Common Sandpiper, Meadow Pipit, Swallow, Chaffinch, Great, Blue and Coal Tits, Raven.

Watendlath from ON *vatn-endi*, end of the lake, and *hlava*, barn
Tarn from ON *tjarn*, small mountain lake
Dock tarn, an upland lake with docks (or water-lilies), from OE *docce*
Thwaite, meadow or clearing, from ON *bveit*
Watendlath and its environs were the setting for Hugh Walpole's *Judith Paris* and *The Herries Chronicle*. In the nineteenth century the hamlet boasted 82 residents; now only five families remain.

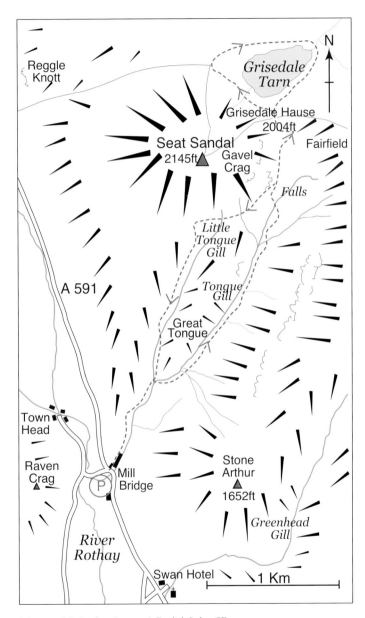

Map: use OS Outdoor Leisure 6, English Lakes SE

WALK 5 A + B
TONGUE GILL & GRISEDALE TARN

**Distance A: 6.5 km / 4 miles
or B: 8 km / 5 miles
Time 3–4 hours**

Park off the A591 at Mill Bridge, N of Grasmere (NY 336096). Cross the A591 and follow bridleway past cottages to gate at beck confluence. Take footbridge to R, then L up valley side, eventually crossing to an old pony track. Continue R to Grisedale Hause, 611m/2,004ft. An optional extra, worthwhile for the views, is to walk clockwise round the tarn. From the Hause, back-track to the junction, then continue R to descend by former pony track to start.

LOOK OUT FOR

April	Golden Saxifrage, Dog Violet, Parsley Fern
May	Starry Saxifrage, Scurvy-grass, Marsh Violet
June	Tormentil, Butterwort, Starry Saxifrage
July	Sundew, Starry Saxifrage, New Zealand Willowherb
August	Heath Milkwort, Lousewort, Sheepsbit
September	Trailing St John's Wort, Bell Heather, Ling
October	Lesser Spearwort, Parsley Fern, Hard Fern

Grisedale Tarn

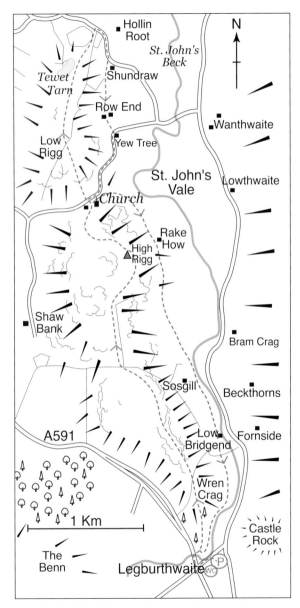

Map: use OS Outdoor Leisure 4, English Lakes North West

WALK 6 ◆ HIGH RIGG & ST JOHN'S VALE

Distance 12 km / 7 ½ miles
Time 4–5 hours

Park in Forest Enterprises
Legburthwaite car park (NY 318191)
off the B5322, Vale of St John, 700m
beyond the A591. Go through gate at
N end of car park, L along lane to main
road, then R beside road for 350m.
Take footpath on R, going L at fork
to climb the ridge above Wren Crag,
continuing along to High Rigg, before
descending to the church of St John-in-
the-Vale (a visit is recommended).
Cross road opposite church and follow
footpath past Tewet Tarn to road. Go
R for 350m to Shundraw Farm taking
footpath to the R of it through fields
past Row End to a metalled road at Yew
Tree Farm. Go R up road for 600m and
just before church take walled path on
L along valley side back to start.

St John's Vale

LOOK OUT FOR

April	Golden Saxifrage, Gorse, Bilberry
May	Bogbean, Tormentil, Heath Milkwort
June	Heath Bedstraw, Broom, Foxglove
July	Lesser Stitchwort, Lousewort, Brooklime
August	Bell Heather, Trailing St John's Wort, Hedge Bedstraw
September	Ling, Sneezewort, Yarrow

Birds include Heron, Mallard,
Meadow Pipit, Wheatear, Willow
Warbler, Jay, Carrion Crow, Rook,
Jackdaw, Pied and Grey Wagtail,
Buzzard.

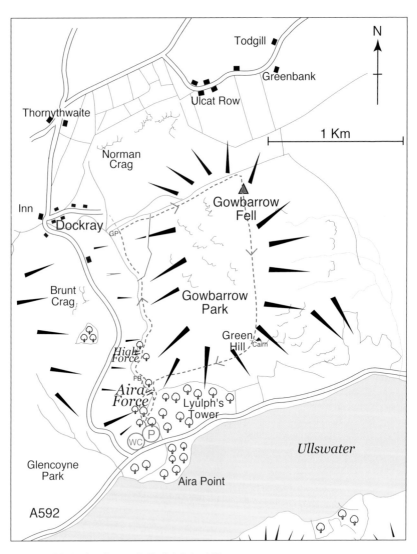

Map: use OS Outdoor Leisure 5, English Lakes NE

WALK 7
GOWBARROW FELL & AIRA FORCE

Distance 8 km / 5 miles
Time 2¹/₂–3 hours

Park at Aira Force National Trust car park (NY 401200). Follow footpath N. Just before footbridge take path to L through woods, bypassing Aira Force, and stone footbridge up to a wooden footbridge. Cross, and continue up opposite side of beck, past High Force to the second crossing wall and guide post. Go R, then over a ladder stile and continue steeply alongside a wall to the summit of Gowbarrow Fell, 481m/1,579ft. From there follow meandering indistinct undulating path S along tops to Green Hill then SW down to Aira Force. View force and return to car park at start.

William Wordsworth knew this valley well, and set his heroic poem 'The Somnambulist' in Aira Force. It starts:

List, ye who pass by Lyulph's Tower
    At eve; how softly then
Doth Aira-force, that torrent hoarse,
    Speak from the woody glen!
Fit music for a solemn vale!
    And holier seems the ground
To him who catches on the gale
The spirit of a mournful tale,
    Embodied in the sound. . . .

Just south of here he was inspired to write, 'I wandered lonely as a cloud . . .'

LOOK OUT FOR

April	Golden Saxifrage, Daffodil, Dog Violet
May	Bilberry, Heath Milkwort, Cotton Grass
June	Cow Wheat, English Stonecrop, Heath Spotted Orchid
July	Bell Heather, Bog Asphodel, Marsh Bedstraw
August	Ling, Sheepsbit, Sneezewort
September	Devil's Bit Scabious, Yarrow, Knapweed
October	Lesser Spearwort, Tormentil, Bell Heather

Birds include Meadow Pipit, Skylark, Kestrel, Buzzard, Cuckoo, Willow Warbler, Wren, Swallow, Swift and others. Red Deer may also be seen.

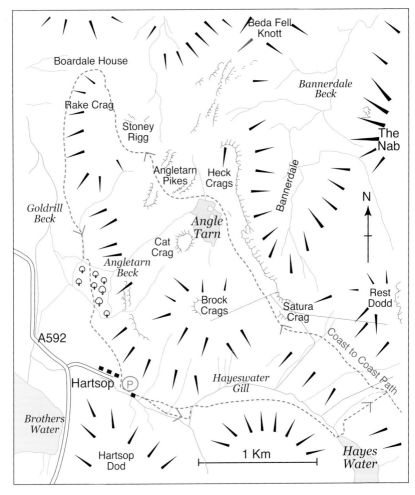

Map: use OS Outdoor Leisure 5, English Lakes NE

WALK 8 ◆ HAYESWATER & ANGLE TARN

Distance 11 km / 7 miles
Time 4–4½ hours

Park at head of Hartsop village (NY 409131). Take bridleway to E from car park for 400m, then bear R along permitted path past ruined corn mill to lead mine wheelpit where path turns sharply to L to regain track. Follow R and R again at fork to cross Hayeswater Gill and up to Hayeswater dam. Recross gill and zig-zag steeply up to join Coast-to-Coast Path NW of The Knott. Follow this L past Satura Crag to Angle Tarn. Continue, skirting Angle Tarn Pikes to Boardale Hause where a bridleway on L leads down to valley floor. At Angle Tarn Beck fork L through Calf Close Wood to start.

The only Golden Eagles breeding in England may be seen by going R at the Coast-to-Coast Path just past The Knott and looking down Riggindale. To see them from the RSPB hide in Riggindale, descend from The Knott down Kidsty Pike to Haweswater shore and take path up S side of Riggindale Beck. Alternately drive down E side of Haweswater and park at end of lake (NY 469107) and follow signs on foot.

LOOK OUT FOR

April	Golden Saxifrage, Spring Sedge, Parsley Fern
May	Starry Saxifrage, Cotton Grass, Butterwort
June	New Zealand Willowherb, Marsh Thistle, Lousewort
July	Starry Saxifrage, Sundew, Water Lobelia
August	Ling, Sheep's Sorrel, Tormentil
September	Bell Heather, Scurvygrass, Devil's Bit Scabious
October	Tormentil, Lesser Spearwort, Autumnal Hawkbit

Birds you may see include Golden Eagle, Buzzard, Kestrel, Peregrine Falcon, Sparrowhawk, Raven, Meadow Pipit, Wren, Wheatear and many others. In May look for Red Deer calves and nursing hinds in valley bottom; in October look (and listen) for Red Deer rut in Bannerdale and The Nab red deer reserve.

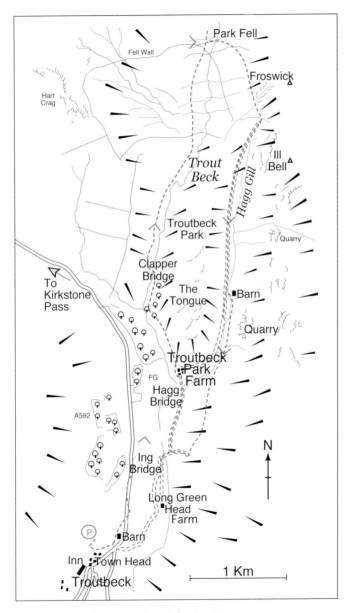

Map: use OS Outdoor Leisure 7, English Lakes SE

WALK 9 ◆ TROUTBECK TONGUE

Distance 12 km / 7½ miles
Time 4½–5½ hours

Park at Troutbeck Town Head lay-by
(NY 415039) on the A592, the
Kirkstone Pass Road. Take lane to E of
road then fork L to cross Ing Bridge and
Hagg Bridge before reaching Troutbeck
Park Farm. Pass in front of buildings,
go R through a gate and continue
up through woods to a stout clapper
bridge. Cross, and continue along the
valley flank. After third wall crossing
over fell wall, bear R, cross beck and
keeping fell wall on R continue along
fell side to join a grassy bridleway, part
of the old Roman Road. Follow for 2km
and at a gate on L, where the bridleway
goes off, cross Hagg Gill, pass an old
quarry, and just before Long Green
Head Farm take the farm track R down
to Ing Bridge, and back to start.

The boggy paths between the clapper
bridge and the fell wall are indistinct.

Troutbeck Park Farm was once owned by
Beatrix Potter who re-introduced here the
old Herdwick breed of sheep. She left it with
13 other farms to the National Trust.

The Ill Bell Ridge to the east of the dale
consists of (from the south):
Yoke (704m/2,309ft), Ill Bell (755m/2,476ft)
and Froswick (719m/2,359ft).

LOOK OUT FOR

April	Golden Saxifrage, Spring Sedge, Coltsfoot
May	Lousewort, Marsh Valerian, Cotton Grass
June	Heath Spotted Orchid, Mountain Saxifrage, Butterwort
July	Marsh Woundwort, Alpine Lady's Mantle, Sundew
August	Scurvygrass, Marsh Bedstraw, Grass of Parnassus
September	Lesser Stitchwort, Water Pepper, Devil's Bit Scabious

Valley birds include Buzzard,
Sparrowhawk, Raven, Swallow,
Pied Wagtail, Meadow Pipit,
Carrion Crow, Jackdaw, Cuckoo,
Willow Warbler, Wren, Chaffinch,
Robin, Wheatear, Long-tailed,
Blue and Great Tits, Green and
Great Spotted Woodpecker, Rook,
Black-headed Gull and Snipe.
Red Deer frequent the Tongue and
the cultivated valley fields during
the winter months; they are most
likely to be seen in early morning
or (less likely) around dusk.

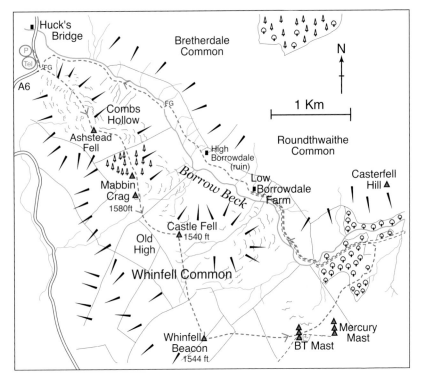

Map: use OS Outdoor Leisure 7, English Lakes SE

WALK 10
WHINFELL BEACON & BORROWDALE

Distance 14.5 km / 9 miles
Time 4½–5 hours

Park at the wide lay-by with telephone
kiosk on the A6 near Huck's Bridge
(NY 553037), 13km/8 miles N of
Kendal. A field gate on the E side of
the road gives access to the steepish
path up Ashstead Fell that continues
past Mabbin Crag and Castle Crag
to Whinfell Beacon. Beyond the
Beacon, almost alongside the tele-
communications mast, take a footpath
L down to the Borrowdale Valley
bottom road. Go L along the road past
Low and High Borrowdale Farms before
the road becomes a farm track. Follow
this back to start.

Westmorland Fell ponies are frequently seen
on Bretherdale Common, the fellside to the
east of Borrow Beck. They roam freely on the
fells throughout the year and are indifferent to
walkers, unless possibly when with young they
feel threatened. As with any other animals
you encounter, including suckler cattle in the
valley bottom, you should pass them quietly
at a respectable distance, preferably avoiding
getting between them and their young.

LOOK OUT FOR

April	Spring Sedge, Cranberry, Bilberry
May	New Zealand Willowherb, Cranberry, Cowberry
June	Heath Bedstraw, Lousewort, Butterwort
July	Butterwort, Sundew, Bog Asphodel
August	Cotton Grass, Grass of Parnassus and Sneezewort
September	Second Flowering of Gorse, Bilberry, Cowberry
October	Yarrow, Lesser Spearwort, Autumnal Hawkbit

Birds that may be seen include
Merlin, Kestrel, Meadow Pipit,
Chaffinch, Wren, Crow, Jackdaw,
Skylark, Sandpiper, Pied and Grey
Wagtails and Stonechat. Arrival
of winter resident Fieldfares and
Redwings in October, and Sand
Martins, Swallows, Willow
Warblers, Chiffchaffs, Cuckoo
and Wheatear in May.

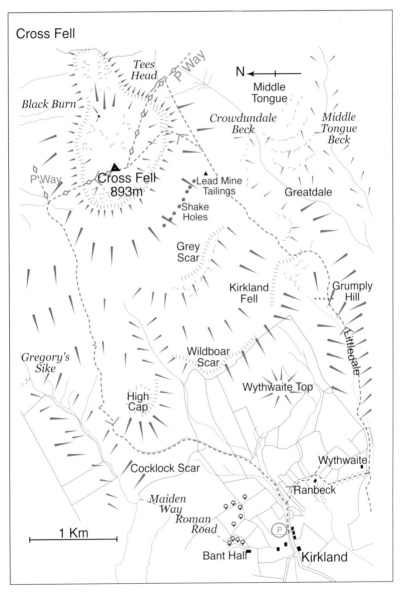

Map: use OS Outdoor Leisure 31, North Pennines Teesdale and Weardale
or OS Pathfinder 578, Appleby-in-Westmorland

WALK 11 ◆ KIRKLAND & CROSS FELL

Distance 14.5 km / 9 miles
Time 4¹/₂–5¹/₂ hours

From the A686, 600m N of
Langwathby, take minor road to
R through Skirwith to Kirkland and
park on the verge beside Kirkland Beck
(NY 650325). Proceed up Garrigill
bridleway for a short distance and
take footpath on R alongside wall to
Ranbeck Farm. Pass ruined barn to R,
then through field gates to join track.
Follow L to Wythwaite Farm, beyond
which take track L up Littledale
skirting Grumply Hill to cross Wildboar
Scar. From here on the footpath is
often indistinct, but well cairned
(compass course 055). After about 17
cairns bear L on compass course 025,
past two more cairns and by the
grassiest route up the boulder field
(look for Fir Clubmoss among boulder
scree) to summit rim between three
cairns. From here bear compass course
320 to Trig Point and shelter. Leave
shelter by cairned Pennine Way,
compass 345, to join the Kirkland–
Garrigill bridleway. Follow this L down
to start.

Wear warm, waterproof and
windproof clothing and stout boots,
and carry a map and compass against
sudden mists or low cloud. When wind
is in the east, beware the turbulent
Helm Wind that can create problems
of balance on exposed rocks or ledges.

LOOK OUT FOR

May	Gorse, Ivy-Leaved Water Crowfoot, Fir Clubmoss
June	Mossy Saxifrage, Alpine Lady's Mantle, Brooklime
July	Tormentil, Heath Bedstraw, Cotton Grass
August	Lesser Stitchwort, Gorse, Water Crowfoot
September	Sneezewort, Yarrow, Knapweed
October	Gorse, Smooth Hawksbeard, Catsear

Birds include Meadow Pipit,
Wheatear, Willow Warbler,
Skylark, Kestrel, Sparrow Hawk,
Lapwing, Curlew, Golden Plover,
Snipe, Ring Ouzel, Wren, Swallow,
Swift, Crow and Chaffinch plus
flocks of immigrant Fieldfares and
Redwings from October onwards
until spring.

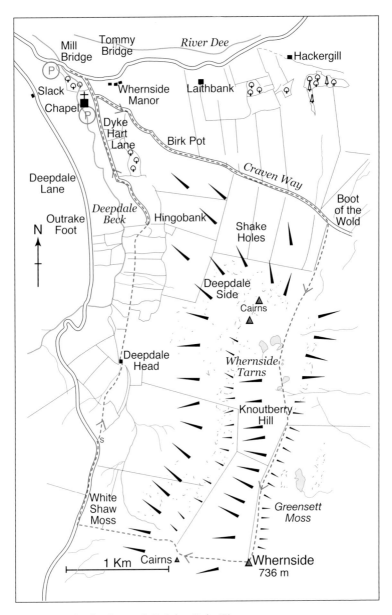

Map: use OS Outdoor Leisure 2, Yorkshire Dales West

WALK 12 ✦ WHERNSIDE

Distance 14.5 km / 9 miles
Time 4¹/₂–5¹/₂ hours

Park on the roadside at Mill Bridge
(SD 721861) on minor road SE
from Dent village). Walk E along road
to join Dyke Hall Lane on R beside
chapel (alternative car parking here,
for a donation). 250m on, dog-leg L
joins Craven Way (bridleway). Follow
it 2.8km to Boot of the Wold. Turn R
and follow wall to end then continue
in same direction to Whernside Tarns
and on to summit ridge of Whernside.
At summit cairn (SD 738815), 736m/
2,419ft, strike due W to follow a wall
down to the Kingsdale road. Follow
road to R for 800m then take footpath
on R past Deepdale Head Farm,
Miregarth and Blake Rigg to join Dyke
Hall Lane, which follow back to start.

LOOK OUT FOR

April	Golden Saxifrage, Town Hall Clock (in Dyke Hall Lane)
May	Spring Sedge, Tormentil, Whitlow Grass
June	Sundew, Cotton Grass, Heath Bedstraw
July	Bell Heather, Cross-Leaved Heath, Lousewort
August	Ling, Lesser Spearwort, Marsh Bedstraw
September	Cowberry (second flowering), Devil's Bit Scabious

Birds to be seen include Meadow
Pipit, Skylark, Lapwing, Curlew,
Golden Plover, Willow Warbler,
Cuckoo, Chaffinch, Pied Wagtail,
Wren, Kestrel, Peregrine Falcon
Swallow, House Martin, Wood
Pigeon, Red Grouse.

Whernside means the farm where millstones (querns) come from. This is the highest of the
Yorkshire Three Peaks, and the others – Ingleborough at 723m/2,372ft and Pen-y-Ghent at
694m/2,277ft – can be seen from the summit. Dentdale is the valley of the River Dee. The
Craven Way is an old drovers' road and packhorse route between Dent and Ingleton. The
section described here is also known as the Great Wold.

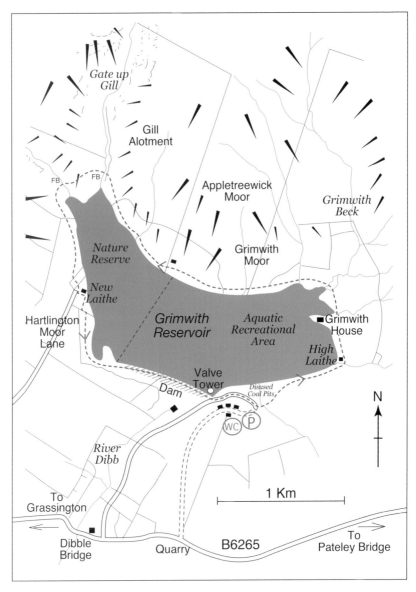

Map: use OS Outdoor Leisure 2, Yorkshire Dales South and West

WALK 13 ◆ GRIMWITH RESERVOIR

Distance 7 km / 4½ miles
Time 2½–3 hours

From the B6225 6km E of Grassington take Reservoir Access track on N side of road and drive to Yorkshire Water car park (SE 063640). Walk E along track through gate. After 300m take footpath to L towards waterside and High Laithe, a restored traditional Dales ling-thatched field barn. Continue along track past Grimwith House and ruined farmhouse to a gate where track ends and footpath starts into a nature reserve. A track, Hartlington Moor Lane, is soon reached and followed to a footpath sign on L. Follow past New Laithe on path across dam back to start.

LOOK OUT FOR

April	Golden Saxifrage, Water Crowfoot, Whitlow Grass
May	Ragged Robin, Tormentil, Cotton Grass
June	Foxglove, Water Forget-me-Not, Marsh Thistle
July	Rose Bay Willowherb, Spear Thistle, Great Burdock
August	Ling, Marsh Bedstraw, Rose Bay Willowherb
September	Lesser Spearwort, Sneezewort, Tormentil

Birds include Short-eared Owl, Partridge, Pheasant, Red Grouse, Snipe, Lapwing, Meadow Pipit, Carrion Crow, Starling, Chaffinch, Goldfinch, Grey Wagtail, Mallard, Wigeon, Teal, Sandpiper, Ringed Plover, Oyster Catcher, Herring Gull, Lesser Black-backed Gull, Grey Lag Goose and Canada Goose, among others.

Grimwith Barn

Grimwith was developed into a 151-hectare/371-acre reservoir by Yorkshire Water in the mid 1970s. It became the second largest inland water body in the Yorkshire and Humberside region. The Yorkshire Dales National Park, the planning authority, in association with English Nature, negotiated access and environmental conditions to preserve the wildlife and the quiet remoteness of the area.

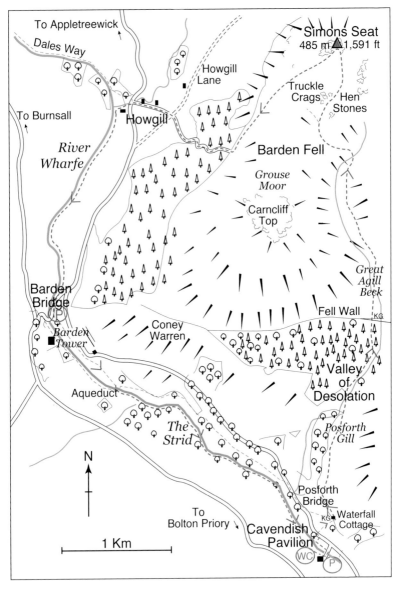

Map: use OS Outdoor Leisure 10, Yorkshire Dales South
or OS Explorer 27, Lower Wharfedale

WALK 14 ◆ BARDEN FELL & STRID WOOD

Distance 14.5 km / 9 miles
Time 4¹/₂–5¹/₂ hours

Off the B6160 near Barden Tower, take Appletreewick road to Barden Bridge; over the bridge park on the wide verge (SE 052574). Cross road and take riverside footpath to viaduct. Cross to W bank of River Wharfe and go through Strid Wood (Site of Special Scientific Interest) past The Strid to Cavendish Pavilion (toilets and refreshments). From Cavendish, cross facing bridge and follow footpath L to cross road up to Waterfall Cottage. Through a kissing gate take the path up the Valley of Desolation, named after a devastating storm in the early nineteenth century, via a plantation to the fell wall. Optional diversions to view waterfalls. A clear easy track leads gently up through the grouse moor to Simon's Seat, 485m/1,591ft on weather-worn millstone grit. From the viewpoint go L (SW) along a cairned track down to Howgill and straight on to join the Dales Way. Follow this L by Wharfeside back to start.

An easy walk on well-made paths with only moderate gradients. An agreement between Yorkshire Dales National Park and the Cavendish Estates (for Bolton Abbey) allows free roaming on fell, but your discretion is expected during grouse nesting and fledgling stages. The Estate is occasionally closed for shooting.

LOOK OUT FOR

March	Golden Saxifrage, Coltsfoot, Primrose
April	Bluebell, Whitlow Grass, Bilberry
May	Crowberry, Cowberry, Heath Bedstraw
June	Climbing Corydalis, Cow Wheat, Cross-Leaved Heath
July	Yellow Pimpernel, New Zealand Willowherb, Lesser Stitchwort
August	Ling, Lesser Stitchwort, Bilberry (second flush)
September	Devil's Bit Scabious, Burnet Saxifrage, Cowberry (reflowering)
October	Cowberry, Water Forget-me-not, Devil's Bit Scabious

Birds include Red Grouse, Skylark, Meadow Pipit and Short-eared Owl on fell; near river Great and Blue Tits, Goldfinch, Chaffinch, Green and Spotted Woodpecker, Moorhen, Mallard, Dipper, Pied and Grey Wagtails, Goosander, Kingfisher and Heron. Adders and lizards may be encountered on moor.

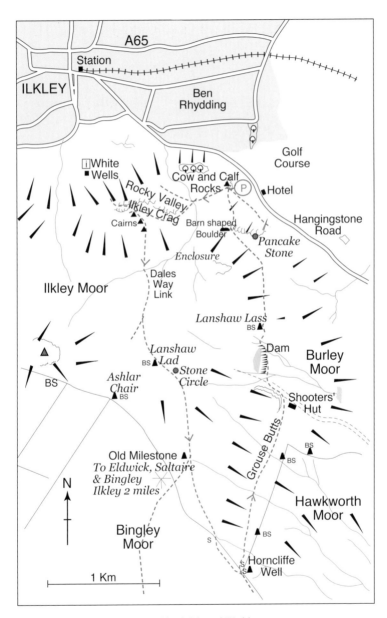

Map: use OS Explorer 27, Lower Wharfedale and Washburn

WALK 15 ◆ ILKLEY MOOR

Distance 11 km / 7miles
Time 4–4¹/₂ hours

Park at the Ilkley Cow and Calf Rocks car park (SE 133467). From there go SW skirting Cow and Calf group above Rocky Valley to join Dales Way link S of Ilkley Crags. Go L along this cairned path ignoring a fork to the R after 1 km, passing Laneshaw Lad, a carved stoop and a cairn on the R, and a Bronze Age stone circle, the Twelve Apostles, on L. 800m on take the indistinct L fork opposite old milestone, then through a wall to Horncliffe Well on L. Take the first of two stiles and continue NNE on Burley Moor. Just past a shooters' shelter go L along a track over a dam, then bearing L continue N along an obvious path past Lanshaw Lass, a boundary stone on L, to a prominent barn-shaped boulder on a scarp 400m W of Pancake Stone. Take path N back to Cow and Calf Rocks and start.

Ilkley is from Illica's *leah*, OE for clearing. Occupied since the Mesolithic (Middle Stone Age), here men hunted and gathered berries, nuts and plants. Neolithic (New Stone Age) men started farming and left more advanced tools. They also erected the stone circles. The warmer Bronze Age brought continental immigrants who left behind rock carvings, mostly cup and ring. The Romans had an important fort here, partly to protect their lead and silver mines to the west, and named it Olicana.

LOOK OUT FOR

April	Golden Saxifrage, Bilberry, Crowberry
May	Cotton Grass, Bilberry, Crowberry
June	Cross-leaved Heath, Bell Heather, Cowberry
July	Ling, Bilberry, Crowberry (fruits)
August	Sundew, Heath Bedstraw, Tormentil
September	Bell Heather, Ling, Cross-leaved Heath
October	Star Moss, Sphagnum Moss, Hard Fern

Birds: Red Grouse, Wheatear, Golden Plover, Ring Ousel, Sandpiper, Meadow Pipit, Kestrel, Curlew, Lapwing and Greylag Geese all breed here.

Cup and ring stone at
Green Crag Slack, Ilkley Moor

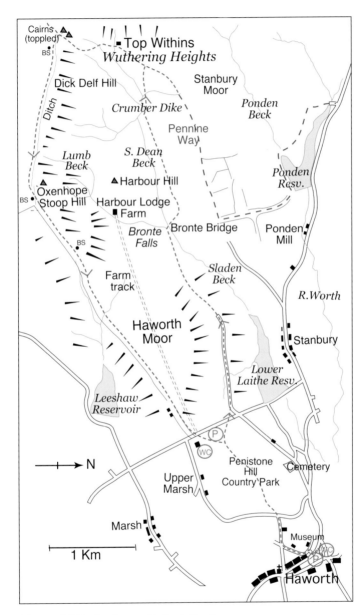

Cairns
(toppled)
BS
Dick Delf Hill
Ditch
Top Withins
Wuthering Heights
Crumber Dike
Stanbury
Moor
*Ponden
Beck*
Pennine
Way
*Lumb
Beck*
*S. Dean
Beck*
Harbour Hill
Oxenhope
BS Stoop Hill
Harbour Lodge
Farm
*Bronte
Falls*
Bronte Bridge
*Ponden
Resv.*
Ponden
Mill
BS
Farm
track
*Sladen
Beck*
R. Worth
Haworth
Moor
Stanbury
*Lower
Laithe Resv.*
*Leeshaw
Reservoir*
N
Penistone
Hill
Country Park
Cemetery
Upper
Marsh
P
WC
Marsh
Museum
WC
1 Km
Haworth

Map: use OS Outdoor Leisure 21, South Pennines

WALK 16
WUTHERING HEIGHTS & HAWORTH MOOR

Distance 12 km / 7¹/₂ miles
Time 4–5 hours

Park in car park at N end of Haworth
village near church and Bronte
Parsonage Museum (SE 028377).
The first half of the walk is generously
signed in both English and Japanese.
From car park take steps up to lane
facing Museum. Go L, then R alongside
churchyard and up a walled lane. Take
the first turning to R, which brings you
to the edge of Penistone Hill Country
Park. Cross road and follow signs for
Bronte Falls and Top Withins, across a
road along a reasonable track to Bronte
Falls. Note inscribed rock. Now follow
well-signed footpath along South Dean
Beck to Pennine Way track, where
turn L for Top Withins (Wuthering
Heights). Beyond here, continue S
along Pennine Way for 700m. At
footbridge over a wide ditch opposite
two toppled cairns, turn L along a
boggy path that follows a ditch to a
wall corner. Bear L following wall past
Leeshaw Reservoir and farm to road.
A short dog-leg L past toilets leads
back to start of walk.

LOOK OUT FOR

April	Golden Saxifrage, Gorse, Cotton Grass
May	Bilberry, Cowberry, Crowberry
June	Lesser Spearwort, Foxglove, Sheep's Sorrel
July	Bell Heather, Cross-Leaved Heath, Cowberry
August	Ling, Sheep's Sorrel, Rose Bay Willowherb
September	Sneezewort, Yarrow, Tormentil
October	Late Heathers, Green Spleenwort, Hard Fern

Birds: Merlin, Kestrel, Peregrine
Falcon, Curlew, Golden Plover,
Wren and Meadow Pipit nest here.
Others to be seen include Red
Grouse, Swallow and, on reservoir,
Canada Geese and Gulls.

Haworth was the home from 1820 of the Bronte family, and hereabouts were the settings for
Emily's *Wuthering Heights*, Charlotte's *Jane Eyre* and Anne's *The Tenant of Wildfell Hall*.

FURTHER READING

Back, P., *The Illustrated Herbal* (Hamlyn, 1987)

Blamey, M. and C. Grey-Wilson, *Illustrated Flora of Britain and Northern Europe* (Hodder & Stoughton, 1994)

Blunt, W., *The Complete Naturalist*, (Collins, 1971)

Bown, D., *RHS Encyclopaedia of Herbs* (Dorling Kindersely, 1995)

Ceres, *The Healing Power of Herbal Teas* (Thorsons, 1984)

Chevallier, A., *Encyclopaedia of Medicinal Plants* (Dorling Kindersley, 1996)

Coombes, A. J., *Dictionary of Plant Names* (Collingridge, 1985)

Culpeper, N., *Culpeper's Complete Herbal* (1699; reprint Wordsworth, 1995))

de Gex., J., *A Medieval Herbal* (Pavilion, 1995)

Dorfler, H. P. and G. Roselt, *Dictionary of Healing Plants* (Blandford, 1989)

Duncan, J. E. and R. W. Robson, *Pennine Flowers* (Dalesman, 1977)

Clapham, A. R., ed., *Upper Teesdale* (Collins, 1978)

Fitter, R. A. and M. Blamey, *Wild Flowers of Britain and Northern Europe* (Collins, 1974)

Gerard, J., *Gerard's Herbal* (reprint Senate, 1994)

Gilmour, J. and M. Walters, *Wild Flowers* (Collins New Naturalist Series, 1954)

Gledhill, D., *The Names of Plants* (Cambridge University Press, 2002)

Gordon, L., *A Country Herbal* (Webb & Bowes, 1980)

Grieve, M., *A Modern Herbal* (Tiger, 1931)

Grigson, G., *The Englishman's Flora* (Phoenix House, 1958)

Grigson, G., *Dictionary of English Plant Names* (Lane, 1973)

Grounds, R., *Ferns* (Readers' Union, 1975)

Halliday, G, *A Flora of Cumbria* (Lancaster University, 1997)

Launert, E., *Edible Medicinal Plants of Britain and Northern Europe* (Country Life, 1981)

Louseley, J. E., *Wild Flowers of Chalk and Limestone* (Collins New Naturalist Series, 1950)

Mabey, R., *Flora Britannica* (Sinclair Stevenson, 1996)

McClintock, D. and R. S. R. Fitter, *Pocket Guide to Wild Flowers* (Collins, 1956)

Grieve, M., *A Modern Herbal* (Cape, 1931)

Merryweather, J. and M. Hill, *The Fern Guide* (Field Studies Council, 1992)

Millward, D., *A Flora of Wensleydale* (Yoredale Nature Society, 1988)

Phillips, R., *Wild Flowers of Britain* (Ward Lock, 1977)

Press, B., *Green Guide: Herbs* (New Holland, 1994)

Raistrick, A. and J. L. Illingworth, *The Face of N.W. Yorkshire* (Dalesman, 1949)

Raven, J. and M. Walters, *Mountain Flowers* (Collins New Naturalist Series, 1956)

Sanecki, K. N., *Complete Book of Herbs* (Macdonald, 1974)

Stearn, W. T., *Botanical Latin* (David & Charles, 1966)

Summerhayes, V. S., *Wild Orchids of Britain* (Collins New Naturalist Series, 1951)

Vickery, R., *A Dictionary of Plant Lore* (Oxford University Press, 1995)

Watts, W. M., *A School Flora* (Longmans, 1905)

INDEX OF PLANT NAMES

This index covers plants in the Directory and the Walks of this volume. Botanical names are given, in parentheses, for Directory plants only.

Adder's Tongue (*Ophioglossum vulgatum*), 85
Angelica, Wild (*Angelica sylvestris*), 37, 95
Archangel, Yellow (*Lamiastrum galeobdolon*), 28
Asphodel, Bog (*Narthecium ossifragum*), 28, 97, 99, 107, 113
Avens, Mountain (*Dryas octopetalla*), 37
Bartsia, Alpine (*Bartsia alpina*), 61
Bartsia, Yellow (*Parentucellia viscosa*), 29
Bedstraw, Heath (*Galium saxatile*), 38, 105, 113, 115, 117, 121, 123
Bedstraw, Hedge (*Galium mollugo*), 38, 105
Bedstraw, Marsh (*Galium palustre*), 39, 107, 111, 117, 119
Bilberry (*Vaccinium myrtilis*), 61, 95, 97, 101, 105, 107, 113, 121, 123, 125
Bindweed, Field (*Convolvulus arvensis*), 62
Bistort, Alpine (*Polygonum viviparum*), 39
Blinks (*Montia fontana*), 40
Bluebell, 121
Bogbean (*Menyanthes trifoliata*), 40, 95, 99, 105
Bracken (*Pteridium aquilinum*), 85
Brooklime (*Veronica beccabunga*), 71, 105, 115
Broom (*Cytisus scoparius*), 29, 105
Broomrape, Common (*Orobanche minor*), 36
Burdock, Lesser (*Arctium minus*), 51
Burdock, Great (*Sanguisorbia officinalis*), 119
Burnet, Great, 51
Butterbur (*Petasites hybridus*), 62
Butterwort (*Pinguicula vulgaris*), 71, 95, 97, 99, 101, 103, 109, 111, 113
Catsear, 115
Cinquefoil, Marsh (*Potentilla palustris*), 52
Clubmoss, Alpine (*Lycopodium alpinum*), 75
Clubmoss, Fir (*Urostachys selago*), 75, 99, 115
Clubmoss, Lesser (*Selaginella selaginoides*), 76
Clubmoss, Stag's Horn (*Lycopodium clavatum*), 76
Coltsfoot, 97, 111, 121
Corydalis, Climbing (*Corydalis claviculata*), 30, 99, 121
Cotton Grass (*Eriophorum angustifolium*), 41, 97, 101, 107, 109, 111, 113, 115, 117, 119, 123, 125

Cow Wheat (*Melanpyrum pratense*), 30, 107, 121
Cowberry (*Vaccinium vitis-idaea*), 63, 113, 117, 121, 123, 125
Cranberry (*Vaccinium oxycoccus*), 63, 95, 113
Cress, Thale (*Arabidopsis thaliana*), 41
Crowberry (*Empetrum nigrum*), 64, 121, 123, 125
Crowfoot, Ivy-Leaved Water, 115
Crowfoot, Water, 115, 119
Daffodil, 97, 107
Dock, Clustered (*Rumex conglomeratus*), 77
Dock, Curled (*Rumex crispus*), 77
Fern, Hard (*Blechnum spicant*), 86, 103, 123, 125
Fern, Parsley (*Cryptogramma crispa*), 86, 99, 103, 109
Forget-Me-Not, Water (*Myosotis scorpioides*), 72, 119, 121
Foxglove (*Digitalis purpurea*), 52, 105, 119, 125
Goosegrass (*Galium aparine*), 42
Gorse (*Ulex europaeus*), 31, 95, 105, 113, 115, 115, 115, 125
Hawkbit, Autumnal, 95, 109, 113
Hawksbeard, Smooth, 97, 115
Heath, Cross-Leaved (*Erica tetralix*), 64, 97, 99, 117, 121, 123, 125
Heather, Bell (*Erica cinerea*), 53, 95, 97, 99, 103, 105, 107, 109, 117, 123, 125
Knapweed (*Centaurea nigra*), 53, 107, 115
Lady's Mantle, Alpine (*Alchemilla alpina*), 31, 111, 115
Ling (*Calluna vulgaris*), 54, 95, 99, 101, 105, 107, 109, 117, 119, 121, 123, 125
Lobelia, Water (*Lobelia dortmanna*), 54, 95, 109
Lousewort (*Pedicularis sylvatica*), 65, 99, 101, 103, 105, 109, 111, 113, 117
Lousewort, Marsh (*Pedicularis palustris*), 65
Lungwort (*Pulmonaria officinalis*), 72
Milkwort, Heath (*Polygala serpyllifolia*), 73, 95, 97, 99, 101, 103, 105, 107
Moss, Feather (*Thuidium tamariscinum*), 78
Moss, Sphagnum (*Sphagnum cymbifolium*), 79, 123
Moss, Star (*Polytrichum commune*), 79, 123
Myrtle, Bog (*Myrica gale*), 80, 95, 101
Nettle, Stinging (*Urtica dioica*), 80

Orchid, Heath Spotted (*Dactyllorhiza maculata*), 66, 101, 107, 111
Orchid, Northern Marsh (*Orchis purpurella*), 55, 95
Orpine (*Sedum telephium*), 66
Pansy, Mountain (*Viola lutea*), 55
Parnassus, Grass of (*Parnassia palustris*), 42, 97, 101, 111, 113
Parsley, Hedge (*Torilis japonica*), 67
Pennywort (*Umbilicis rupestris*), 43
Pennywort, Marsh (*Hydrocotyle vulgaris*), 43
Pepper, Water (*Polygonum hydropiper*), 44, 99, 101, 111
Pimpernel, Bog (*Anagalis tenella*), 67, 95
Pimpernel, Yellow (*Lysimachia nemorum*), 32, 101, 121
Plantain, Hoary (*Plantago media*), 81
Plantain, Ratstail (*Plantago major*), 81
Plantain, Ribwort (*Plantago lanceolata*), 82
Plantain, Sea (*Plantago maritima*), 82
Polypody (*Polypodium vulgare*), 87
Primrose, 121
Ragged Robin (*Lychnis flos-cuculi*), 68, 119
Redshank (*Polygonum maculosa*), 68
Rosemary, Bog (*Andromeda polifolia*), 56
Rose Root (*Sedum rosea*), 32
Rush, Soft (*Juncus effusus*), 83
St John's Wort, Trailing (*Hypericum humifusum*), 33, 103, 105
Sandwort, Fine-Leaved (*Minuartia tenuifolia*), 44
Sandwort, Three-Veined (*Moehringia trinervia*), 45
Saxifrage, Burnet, 121
Saxifrage, Golden (*Chrysosplenium oppositofolium*), 33, 97, 99, 101, 103, 105, 107, 109, 111, 117, 119, 121, 123, 125
Saxifrage, Mossy (*Saxifraga hypnoides*), 45, 115
Saxifrage, Starry (*Saxifraga stellaris*), 46, 103, 109
Saxifrage, Yellow Mountain (*Saxifraga aizoides*), 34, 97, 111
Scabious, Devil's Bit (*Sucissa pratensis*), 73, 95, 97, 99, 107, 109, 111, 117, 121
Scurvygrass (*Cochlearia officinalis*), 46, 103, 109, 111
Sedge, Spring (*Carex caryophyllea*), 34, 101, 109, 111, 113, 117
Sheepsbit (*Jasione montana*), 74, 103, 107
Sneezewort (*Achillea ptarmica*), 47, 95, 97, 101, 105, 107, 113, 115, 119, 125
Sorrel, Mountain (*Oxyria digyna*), 83

Sorrel, Sheep's (*Rumex acetosella*), 84, 99, 109, 125
Spearwort, Lesser (*Ranunculus flammula*), 35, 95, 97, 99, 101, 103, 107, 109, 113, 117, 119, 125
Speedwell, Heath (*Veronica officinalis*), 56
Spleenwort, Green, 125
Stitchwort, Lesser (*Stellaria graminae*), 47, 105, 111, 115, 121
Stitchwort, Marsh (*Stellaria palustris*), 48
Stitchwort, Wood (*Stellaria nemorum*), 48
Stonecrop, English (*Sedum anglicum*), 49, 107
Sundew (*Drosera rotundifolia*), 49, 95, 97, 101, 103, 109, 111, 113, 117, 123
Sundew, Oblong-Leaved (*Drosera intermedia*), 50, 95
Thistle, Creeping (*Cirsium arvense*), 57
Thistle, Marsh (*Cirsium palustre*), 57, 109, 119
Thistle, Spear (*Cirsium vulgare*), 58, 119
Toadflax, Ivy-Leaved (*Cymbalaria muralis*), 58
Tormentil (*Potentilla erecta*), 35, 95, 97, 99, 101, 103, 105, 107, 109, 109, 115, 117, 119, 123, 125
Town Hall Clock, 117
Tutsan (*Hypericum androsaemum*), 36
Valerian, Marsh (*Valeriana dioica*), 69, 111
Violet, Dog, 99, 103, 107
Violet, Marsh (*Viola palustris*), 59, 103
Whitlow Grass, 119, 121
Willowherb, Marsh (*Epilobium palustre*), 69, 97
Willowherb, New Zealand (*Epilobium brunescens*), 70, 97, 103, 109, 113, 121
Willowherb, Rose Bay (*Chamaenerion angustifolium*), 59, 119, 125
Woundwort, Marsh (*Stachys palustris*), 60, 111
Yarrow (*Achillea millefolium*), 50, 105, 107, 113, 115, 125